Crochet for Beginners 2021

A Complete Step By Step Guide with Picture illustrations to Learn Crocheting the Quick & Easy Way

Contents

Introduction

Chapter 1: How to Read and Understand Crochet

Chapter 2: Crocheting Supplies

Chapter 3: Types of Crochet

Chapter 4: How to Crochet for Right-Handers

Chapter 5: How to Crochet for Left-Handers

Chapter 6: Tips and Tricks to Crocheting

Chapter 7: Choosing a Crochet Pattern

Chapter 8: Easy and Fun Crochet Patterns for Beginners

Conclusion

© Copyright 2021 - All rights reserved.

The following eBook is reproduced below with the goal of providing information that is as accurate and reliable as possible. Regardless, purchasing this eBook can be seen as consent to the fact that both the publisher and the author of this book are in no way experts on the topics discussed within and that any recommendations or suggestions that are made herein are for entertainment purposes only. Professionals should be consulted as needed prior to undertaking any of the action endorsed herein.

This declaration is deemed fair and valid by both the American Bar Association and the Committee of Publishers Association and is legally binding throughout the United States.

Furthermore, the transmission, duplication, or reproduction of any of the following work including specific information will be considered an illegal act irrespective of if it is done electronically or in print. This extends to creating a secondary or tertiary copy of the work or a recorded copy and is only allowed with express written consent from the Publisher. All additional rights reserved.

The information in the following pages is broadly considered to be a truthful and accurate account of facts, and as such any inattention, use or misuse of the information in question by the reader will render any resulting actions solely under their purview. There are no scenarios in which the publisher or the original author of this work can be in any fashion deemed liable for any hardship or damages that may befall them after undertaking information described herein.

Additionally, the information in the following pages is intended only for informational purposes and should thus be thought of as universal. As befitting its nature, it is presented without assurance regarding its prolonged validity or interim quality. Trademarks that are mentioned are done without written consent and can in no way be considered an endorsement from the trademark holder.

Introduction

Crocheting is an old favorite pastime, pretty much like stamp collecting, and coin collecting. These hobbies were incredibly popular back in the day when electronic gadgets didn't get in the way of our leisure time. Often times, when we imagine crochet, we think of our grandmothers crocheting a table runner or placemats in her rocking chair. At a certain time, it seemed as though the world had lost its interest in arts and craft. However, with blogs and social media accounts that focus on craft, such as *Diply*, *Pinterest*, *Buzzfeed* and *Tastemade*, crocheting and other long-forgotten handicrafts are making a comeback, albeit with a fresher twist compared to what our grandmothers used to do. Crocheting as we see it today was not how it was done back then.

A quick search on *Instagram* will show you plenty of ways to make cool crop tops, comfortable shoes, bags, phone covers, dream catchers, as well as cute dolls. Thanks to its new techniques and tools, crocheting has turned into a trendy and modern craft.

So, if you've ever looked at a crocheting video and thought, *I want to do that too*, then you're in luck! Because in this book, we will teach you the fundamentals of crocheting, starting from the how-to's, know-hows, techniques, and patterns.

If you are new to the art of crocheting, going through the number of hooks, stitches, yarns, and patterns may all seem confusing and even overwhelming at first, but this book will take you on a journey that will uncover all the basics, so you don't feel overwhelmed.

In this book, we will learn a little bit about the history of crocheting as well as the supplies that you will need. We will also discuss basic crochet patterns, and how to crochet effectively. This book aims to help you firmly grasp the basics of crochet whether it's selecting the right supplies, what hook size conversions are required as beginners, standard yarn weights and figuring out what specialist abbreviations and symbols are. At the very end, we will also investigate how to complete a variety of basic crochet stitches!

Chapter 1: How to Read and Understand Crochet

To pick up or start any kind of new craft or hobby, one must first get acquainted with the language of that particular art. It's the same case with crocheting – before attempting to read crochet patterns, you must first develop an understanding of the craft. This is fairly similar to looking up recipes. When we first set eyes on a recipe, we scan the list of ingredients, the cooking time, as well as instructions to see if it is something that we can attempt based on our prior skill level. It is the same with crochet patterns. To give you an idea, here are a couple of factors you should keep in mind before you sit down to crochet:

1- Level of Difficulty

The level of difficulty is one of the first aspects to consider. Almost all crochet patterns are rated either *beginner*, *easy*, *intermediate*, or *experienced*. Beginner patterns are, of course, suitable for those who are new to crocheting as it requires basic stitches that are simple to create simple. If you're a beginner, start with easier stitches and work your way up. Once you've learned the ropes, you can move up to more advanced patterns.

2- Check the Gauge

Checking the gauge on your patterns ensures that your outcome is the right size. After this, you would also need to count your stitches as you go along so you can keep track of how many stitches there are in each row.

3- Practice

Like every form of art or skill, excelling at crocheting requires patience, perseverance, and practice. You will struggle at first – this is precisely why you must start with beginner patterns to grasp the basics. But as you continue crocheting more and more, you will eventually get the hang of it, and will be to attempt more advanced patterns in no time.

Crochet Terms and Abbreviations

Crochet patterns use specific codes, and no, they aren't used to confuse you! These codes help along the process, allowing users to understand patterns much better and faster.

Practicing beginner crochet patterns will help you memorize each code until it eventually becomes second nature to you. Here is a list of common abbreviations that you will find while crocheting patterns. These codes enable users to better understand things and make pattern books easier to follow. Keep this list handy for when you are crocheting and if you come across a term that's not on this list, inspect your pattern chart for more insight and add it to this list:

Abbreviation	Meaning
Approx.	Approximately
Beg	Begin(ning)
Bet	Between
Blp	Back Loop Only
Bp	Back Post
Cc	Contrast Color
Ch	**Chain Stitch**
Dc	**Double Crochet**
Dec	Decrease(S)(D)(Ing)
Dtr	Double Treble Crochet
Flp	Front Loop Only
Foll	Follow(Ing)
Fp	Front Post
Hdc	**Half Double Crochet**
Inc	Increase(S)(D)(Ing)
Mc	Main Color
Pat	Pattern
Rem	Remaining
Rep	Repeat
Rib	Ribbing
Rs	Right Side
Sc	**Single Crochet**
Sl St	**Slip Stitch**
St(S)	Stitch(Es)
Tog	Together
Tr	**Treble Crochet**
Ws	Wrong Side
Yo	**Yarn Over Hook**

How to Read Crochet Pattern Instructions

Once you've familiarized yourself with these abbreviations, your next task is to understand the symbols included in the world of crocheting. These symbols or special characters represent clarifications, as well as repetitions in patterns or specific directions. Understanding them is vital to create patterns and develop your skills.

Symbol	Meaning
( )	This symbol is known as *parentheses*. It is used to signify repetitiveness in an action or a stitch. If you come across this sign, you are meant to repeat a stitch in succession. This symbol is typically followed by a number indicating the number of stitches you have to make. This pattern can also be used to signify a group of directions, all using the same specific stitch.
[ ]	These square brackets indicate that you must repeat a stitch pattern. This is required when working in correspondence with a parenthesis. On the other hand, it can also be used to clarify information.
{ }	This symbol is used to indicate repetitive instructions, often ones worked within another set of bracketed directions.
* • ♦ †	Asterisks, bullet points, diamonds, plus signs, and other special characters indicate that the person crocheting must repeat the series of stitches.

To help you understand the symbols mentioned above and how to follow them, here are some working examples:

Example 1:

Row 1: With size H hook, ch 15, sc in 2nd ch from hook and in each ch across, turn. (14 sc)

1. Here, you need to stitch the first row using a size H crochet hook.
2. Make 15 chain stitches.
3. Create a single crochet in the second chain stitch from the hook.
4. Create each chain stitch across, then turn the piece.

    (A repetition of 14 single crochet stitches is required in the first row.)

Example 2:

Row 2: ch 1, 2 sc in first sc, sc in each rem sc across to last sc, 2 sc in last sc, turn. (16 sc)

1. Begin the second row with a chain stitch.
2. Make two single crochets in the previous row's single crochet stitch.
3. Make single crochet stitch in every single crochet on the first row till you reach the final one.
4. Last single crochet in that row, make two single crochets then turn the piece

    (There are 16 single crochet stitches in the first row).

Example 3:

(dc in next sc, ch 2, skip next two sc) twice

1. Parentheses indicate that you must repeat the instructions according to the number of times mentioned.
2. Create a double crochet stitch in the next single crochet.
3. Next, make two chain stitches.
4. Then skip the next two single crochets from the previous row.

5. All of above mentioned steps need to be repeated.

   Once completed twice, you can then move on to the next set of instructions.

Rounds and Rows

The examples mentioned above are stitches that require you to work in rows, meaning you simply have to continue stitching straight across. There will be times when you would need to work in rounds or in a circle. When working with rows, simply turn your piece each time you reach the end of the row. This will create a turning chain, then you can continue working again across the top of that specific row and create another new row. When you work in rounds, you are stitching in a spiral which means you are not required to turn your piece around - you only need to continue rotating. 'RND' is usually the abbreviation for round stitches which is usually shown at the start of each direction. When you see 'Row', this means you need to be crocheting in a row.

How to Read Crochet Pattern Symbols and Charts

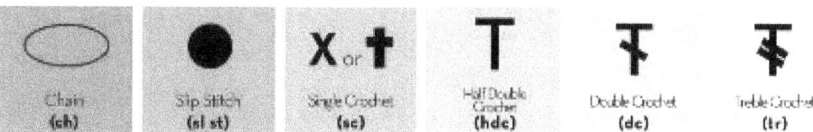

With written instructions, you are likely to find a crochet design in the form of a chart containing more symbols. The symbols are a lot easier to understand and read. Since this book is for beginners, the symbols have been simplified as shown above. This will only show you basic crochet stitches that you'll need to know as a beginner.

Don't worry about not understanding the symbols and abbreviations described here. This information is for you to know and, while it is important, most people who crochet prefer referring to charts.

Single crochets, chain stitches, slip stitches, as well as half double crochets, double crochets, and treble crochets, are all stitches that will make up at least 90% of your stitching repertoire and each of these will be indicated clearly.

The starting point of any design is typically indicated using a black triangle △ or similar, and it is usually accompanied by a row of chain stitches.

Chapter 2: Crocheting Supplies

With any craft, you will always need the appropriate tools to get the job done right. No proper tools, no work of art. In this chapter, we will look at the necessary tools needed to craft any kind of crocheting pattern, whether you are working with a beginner, intermediate, or advanced pattern.

To craft successfully, you will need:

A Crochet Hook

A crochet hook is practically the most important tool of all. Having no hook is like having no camera to take pictures. This tool allows you to create loops in the yarn and interlock these loops into stitches. The crochet hook has a pointy hook end to make it easier for you to insert yarns and hook them. It also has a slanted groove underneath that enables folks to pull loops through easily.

These hooks are made using a variety of materials with the most common being aluminum, wood, and plastic. They also come in various sizes depending on the kind of yarn you're using. For beginners, it is recommended you start crocheting using a basic aluminum crochet hook that is mid-range in size. This allows the beginner to acquire greater control when stitching and looping.

Yarn

The second most important item on the list is yarn. Without it, one can obviously not crochet. The composition of the yarn can vary depending on the crochet project. Yarn is typically made from spun organic fibers that are derived from alpaca and wool. Both these materials are great in providing warmth and elasticity.

Synthetic fibers such as acrylics are also used as an alternative. For beginners, you want to use yarn that is easy to work with, so go for yarn that comes in light, solid colors rather than those with multi-colored strands. This is crucial because it will help you distinguish your stitches as you go about learning different types of stiches.

As a beginner, you also want to use worsted weight yarn. This is a type of medium-weight yarn that is very versatile and extremely easy to work with. This yarn is perfect for creating large blankets and small Japanese amigurumi toys.

Scissors

Almost all craft projects require scissors. You will require it to snip yarn or loose threads for stitching purposes. There are no special scissors for crocheting, but you do want to get a pair of reliable quality scissors. It is advisable you get a pair with a sharp pointed end. Make sure the pointed end is small enough to make quick, clean, and precise cuts. Dressmaking scissors are not recommended as they make it harder to cut with precision.

Crochet Hook Size Conversion Chart

You should be aware of all the different kinds of hooks available for crocheting. This will help you in selecting the correct yarn type. Most hooks already have their metric millimeters stamped on them, so it makes figuring out the hook sizes much easier. The hook size must correspond with the thickness of the yarn. The thicker the yarn, the thicker hook diameter you will need. As for thinner yarns, you can work with thinner hooks of course.

Here is a simple conversion chart for you to compare the metric measurements between UK and US crochet hook sizes. This will make it easier for you to select a yarn according to the diameter. Keep in mind that hook sizes may vary depending on the manufacturer, hence this chart is a simple guide for you to get started.

Metric (millimeters)	UK Size	US Size
2 mm	14	-
2.25 mm	13	B-1
2.5 mm	12	-
2.75 mm	-	C-2
3 mm	11	-
3.25 mm	10	D-3
3.5 mm	9	E-4
3.75 mm	-	F-5
4 mm	8	G-6
4.5 mm	7	7
5 mm	6	H-8
5.5 mm	5	I-9
6 mm	4	J-10
6.5 mm	3	K-10.5
7 mm	2	-
7 mm	2	-
9 mm	00	M/N-13
10 mm	000	N/P-15

Standard Crochet Yarn Weights Chart

Names associated with crochet yarns may also vary in the UK and the US, just like the crochet hooks. It also varies according to the manufacturer. Moving further, beginners find is the usage of 'yarn weight,' which does not mean the weight of the ball of yarn but rather the thickness of the thread. Of course, once you know, it is relatively easy.

In crocheting, the thicker the yarn, the heavier the weight. Once you get acquainted with this idea, it will be easy to understand why it is done this way. The yarn is categorized according to specific weights to make it easier for beginners to know what crochet hook to use and how big the stitches need to be.

US Yarn Weight Name	UK Yarn Weight Name	Gauge Range ('sts' - stitches) per 4 inches	Crochet Hook Range (millimeters)
0 / Lace	2-ply	32 - 42 sts	1.5 mm - 2.25 mm
1 / Super Fine	3-ply / Sport / Baby	21 - 32 sts	2.25 mm - 3.5 mm
2 / Fine	4-ply / Baby	16 - 20 sts	3.5 mm - 4.5 mm
3 / Light	DK / Light Worsted	12 - 17 sts	4.5 mm - 5.5 mm
4 / Medium	Aran / Worsted	11 - 14 sts	5. 5 mm - 6.5 mm
5 / Bulky	Chunky / Rug	8 - 11 sts	6.5 mm – 9mm
6 / Super Bulky	Super Chunky	7 - 9 sts	9 mm – 15 mm

US & UK Yarn Weight Names

To fully comprehend the table shown above, here is a description of each column:

US Yarn Weight Name & UK Yarn Weight Name

These two titles refer to the yarn weight in each country. In the US, measurements are relatively simple to understand with numbers that indicate thickness, but in the UK, the term 'ply' often follows the weights mentioned.

Ply is just another term for 'strand,' so the number you see beforehand is the number of strands that need to be twisted together to create a thread of yarn. For instance, a 2-ply yarn would require two strands to create the yarn, while a 4-ply yarn would need a total of four strands. The higher the ply, the stronger it is, with more density, durability, and elasticity.

Gauge Range & Crochet Hook Range

In this column, the number indicates how many stitches a person is required to make for every four inches of crochet piece. This is a wide estimation. Each crochet person has their own way of performing stitches depending on the level of tightness. The chart suggests the range of stitches that the yarn weight can stitch up to. When looking at that column, you must also learn what *gauge* means.

In crocheting, gauge refers to the tension needed to produce a piece in the correct size. Simply stated, the higher the hook size, the smaller the gauge range and higher the weight of the yarn would be. For instance, if you are crocheting using chunky yarn, you would only need between eight to eleven stitches every four inches. You will also need a bigger crochet hook to handle the weight of the yarn.

The table given here is a rough guide that will help you select the right hook according to the gauge for your pattern. It is extremely crucial to work with the correct gauge, especially when you are creating clothing, or else the finished product may not fit well or turn out to be the appropriate size. Most yarn manufacturers make our lives easier by listing both the 'stitches' and 'rows' under their gauge information on yarn labels. This suggests the number of stitches the yarn will be able to complete in a four by four section, and it also tells you how many rows the yarn will be able to make.

Most patterns also provide this information. For instance, you would see a pattern with *16 sts and 14 rows in a 4" square*. The best way to go about this is to make a 4-inch swatch sample and practice your gauge on the stitch pattern before you begin your project. To accomplish this, first look at the yarn weight, followed by the hook size, then the stitch pattern, and finally the gauge information. When you use the correct materials, test it out by completing a 4-inch swatch using the number of stitches specified in the pattern, both across as well as rows down. Next, count the number of stitches and rows in your sample. If you have completed too many rows and stitches, this means you have worked too tightly. To rectify this, a bigger hook may be used to manage the quantity of stitches.

As always, practicing your crocheting is key until you are able to achieve the correct gauge for your patterns.

Chapter 3: Types of Crochet

When we talk about yarn, plenty of people assume yarn is only meant for knitting. Not to mention, many people think knitting and crocheting are the same. Knitting and crocheting have a number of distinctions, especially when it comes to the tools needed to crochet.

Crocheting has its very own finishes, tools, and techniques, and none of this can be achieved through knitting. In Europe, crocheting began to grow in the early nineteenth century, and at that point, it was known as 'shepherd's knitting.' People found this name befitting because crochet seemed like a cheap alternative to purchasing expensive cloth and lace. With the rule of Queen Victoria, crocheting was made popular thanks to her as she was found purchasing Irish lace crochet items from the people of Ireland during the potato famine. Queen Victoria also picked up crocheting herself which popularized the craft throughout England.

Crochet is not only historic in this sense, but it was also a lifesaver. Many poor families were pulled out of starvation because of the potato famine by crocheting. They used their skills to create items which eventually helped them earn enough to migrate to America. In the 1900s, Irish folks landed in the US bringing with them their crocheting skills. During the war in the 1950s, crocheting was used for making items such as under-helmet caps and nets for soldiers. It was also used by women to embellish dresses and hats, particularly when they did not have access to money and resources. During the 1960s, it was all the rage for women to have crochet fabric and they began crocheting their own pantsuits and shift dresses.

The rise of crocheting rose in popularity in the 1970s as granny squares made their debut in dresses, jackets, and hooded sweatshirts that were made entirely out of these motifs. Next came the 1980s, and there was a full-blown rise in crochet-use in fashion from crochet cardigans, to fete style toys. Sometime in the 1990s, crocheting dwindled, but as explained earlier in the book, with the internet and

Instagram and other social media platforms, crocheting is back with a modern makeover for all things stylish, from kid's toys to home accessories, to clothing items for both women and men. As beginners, it is also good to know the different types of crochet that exists in our world. Take note that crocheting was not a thing in Europe or America. Different variations existed in different parts of the world to be used for a variety of uses from bags to traditional headgear, clothing, bracelets, adornments, as well as home decor.

Here is a list of 21 well-known crocheting types that still exist in the world and are being practiced everywhere:

1. Amigurumi Crochet

This is the most popular form of crochet, and its country of origin is Japan. Amigurumi refers to the art of creating small, stuffed toys or objects from crocheted yarn. Ami means to crochet or even to knit, whereas nuigurumi refers to stuffed dolls. Whenever you see a doll or toy made of yarn, it is most likely amigurumi. Many popular culture items have been used to make amigurumi such as Hello Kitty, Mario Brothers, Pokemon, and Winnie the Pooh.

Items made using Amigurumi crochet:

Children's toys

2. Aran Crochet

This type of crochet is usually cabled or ribbed. It has its roots in Celtic culture and features interlocking cables. It is often the choice of crochet used for making bigger items such as scarves, sweaters, and beanies. If you see the word 'Aran' in your patterns, be careful because Aran is also used to describe the weight of yarn. Cozy blankets and throws are usually made using Aran crochet.

Items made using Aran crochet:

- Blankets
- Jackets
- Coats
- Scarves
- Throws

3. Bavarian Crochet

This Bavarian type of crochet is a vintage crochet stitch, and it is traditionally used in rounds. The resulting piece is often a thick fabric that procures for smooth and blended color changes compared to sharp color changes such as the ones commonly seen in a granny square. With Bavarian crochet, you will work in two parts. The first part is the base of clusters whereas the second part is followed by a row of shells. The Bavarian crochet is the fancier cousin to the granny square.

Items made using Bavarian crochet:
- Blankets
- Shawls
- Tabletop covers

4. Bosnian Crochet

This type of crochet has a knit-like fabric and is quite dense in nature. It is crocheted using a slip stitch and crocheted in different parts from the row before. Bosnian crochet also uses a different type of hook, conveniently called Bosnian crochet hook which you can buy, but using regular hooks can work just as well. This type of crochet is called Shepherd's knitting since it also looks like knitted fabrics.

Items made using Bosnian crochet:

- Scarves
- Beanies
- Socks
- Hand gloves

5. Bullion Crochet

This crochet is a specialized stitch and is achieved using a combination of multiple yarn wraps on a long crochet hook. The result is a distinctive roll stitch which appears quite unique too. Motifs are usually made using bullion crochet, and it results in a uniform, thick, and round motif style piece.

Items made using Bullion crochet:

Stiff items such as placemats
Motifs for decoration

6. Broomstick Crochet

Also known as jiffy lace, broomstick crochet is a type of vintage crochet stitch, which is made with a traditional crochet hook. The resulting stitches are formed around a long and wide object such as broomstick handle, which is how it gets its name. Modern people who crochet use larger crochet hooks or even thick dowels when doing a broomstick crochet. This type of crochet is an excellent skill to learn and master as its final product is very beautiful and unique.

Items made using Broomstick crochet:

   Delicate shawls
   Throw blankets for decoration

7. Bruges Crochet

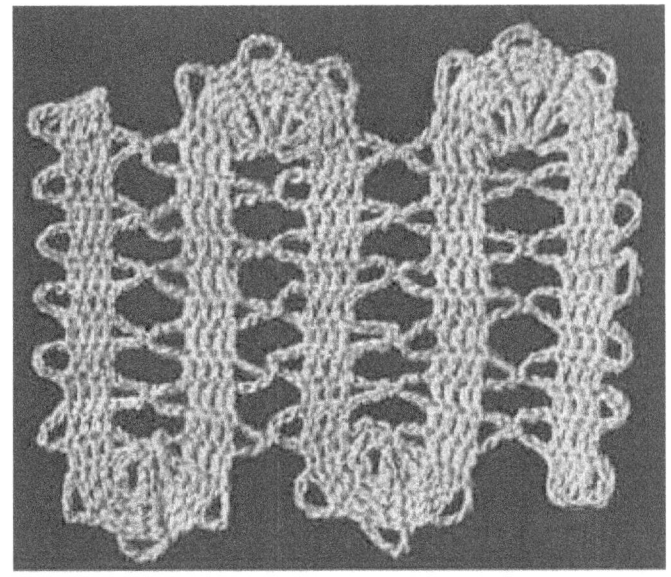

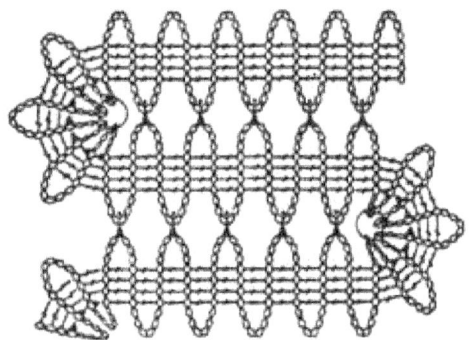

Ribbons of crochet can be created using bruges crochet. These ribbons are then crocheted together, and the results show an intricate lace pattern. This is also the most common type of crochet used in home decor items.

Items made using Bruges crochet:

    Intricate shawls
    Embellishments for clothing
    Table mats

8. Clothesline Crochet

In this crochet style, traditional crochet stitches are done over a clothesline or thick rope or even thick twine to make baskets, and circular mats to hold their shape. This type of crocheting can be traced back to Africa and Nepal.

Items made using clothesline crochet:

    Baskets
    Mats
    Structural wall hangings

9. Clones Lace Crochet

This type of crochet is associated with the Irish lace crochet. It was created to be an alternative to the Irish lace crochet because it's easier and quicker to make than the Irish needlepoint lace. The clones knot used for this type of crocheting requires a unique crochet skillset. Clones lace is a very practical crochet style, and it was commonly used during wars since it was quick and fast to make.

Items made using clones lace crochet:

Open weave scarves
Delicate dresses and tops

10. Cro-hook Crochet

This uniquely named crochet is created using a double-ended hook to create double-sided crochet. This enables you to make stitches on or off at either end of the crochet piece, and this piece does not have a wrong or right side to work on. Because of its nature, this type of crochet is called the Cro-hook or the Cro-knit. This type of crochet closely resembles the Tunisian crochet and is an excellent option if you're working with colors that aren't manageable with other types of crochet.

Items made using clones lace crochet:
- Washcloths
- Scarves
- Baby blankets

11. Filet Crochet

This style is created using chain rows and double crochet stitches. What you get is a grid-like pattern wherein the squares are either filled or not filled, and the negative space is usually there to create images with the pieces. The wonderful thing about this type of crochet is that you can go full-on creative and embed images using empty or full squares of fabric.

Items made using filet crochet:

Baby blankets
Jackets and kimonos
Handbags
Cushions

12. Finger Crochet

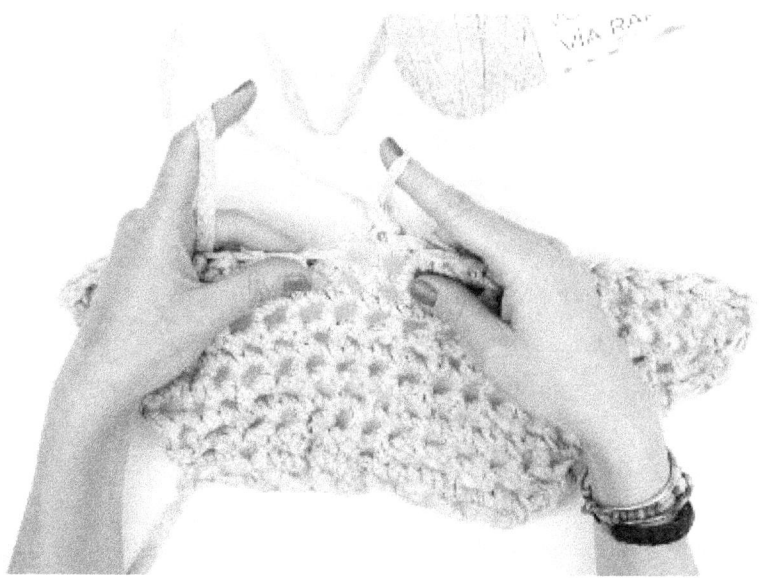

This type of crochet is called as such because it does not require hooks. It is similar to finger knitting. It's basically hand fabric which you can use to weave crochet stitches. This is a fun crochet to do when you are a beginner, but the resulting piece has loose tension which is probably why people move on to hooks to make more versatile projects.

Items made using finger crochet:
- Simple string bags
- Basic scarves

13. Freeform Crochet

This type of crochet is called freeform because there is no pattern or plan to follow. It is entirely up to the person crocheting to create something. This type of crochet is very artistic and organic, making it an excellent option for beginners. However, if you find yourself struggling without instructions or even a plan, then it's best to avoid freeform and follow crochet pieces with patterns.

Items made using freeform crochet:

    One-off clothing items
    Art pieces

14. Hairpin Crochet

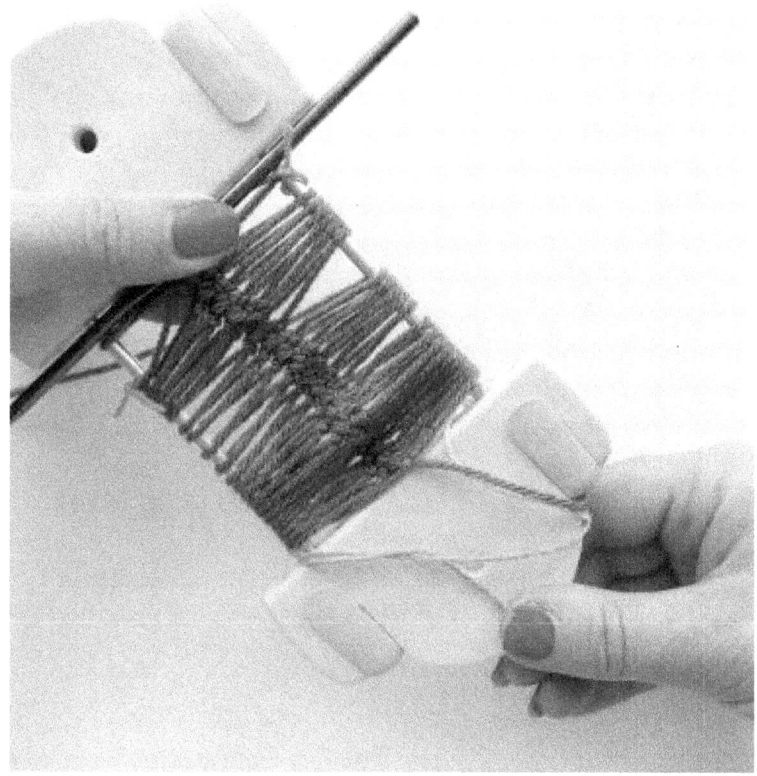

Like the broomstick crochet, the hairpin crochet is made using the traditional crochet hook, but instead of a broomstick, the piece is held taut using thin metal rods. In earlier times, this technique used actual hairpins which is how it got its name. The resulting piece is unique and beautiful.

Items made using hairpin crochet:
- Delicate scarves
- Shawls
- Wraps

15. Micro Crochet

The micro crochet is a modern crochet style and is made using very fine yarn thread with extremely fine or small crochet hooks. It is a very delicate crocheting process and is great for those who are patient and like dainty and small things.

Item made using micro crochet:

Tiny things for dollhouses
Embellishments
Talisman

16. Overlay Crochet

This technique is also quite unique where a base of crochet stitches is made, and then other stitches are added to the top to create a raised pattern. This crocheting technique is more advanced, and it brings many possibilities for you to create intricate pieces.

Items made using overlay crochet:

- Potholders
- Wall hangings
- Handbags

17. Pineapple Crochet

The pineapple crochet is considered more of a general stitch and shape rather than a technique. You can use this crochet to create scarves, doilies, and certain types of clothing. This stitch was very popular in the 1970s, and once you know how to spot this type of stitch, you will be seeing it everywhere.

Items made using pineapple crochet:

- Dresses
- Tops
- Shawls
- Wraps

18. Stained Glass Crochet

The stained glass crochet could be mistaken for the overlay crochet. However, it is different because the top part is normally made using only black yarn to accentuate the colors and create the stained glass effect. What you get is a very striking crochet pattern.

Items made using stained glass crochet:

Thick, sturdy items
Winter scarves
Handbags

19. Symbol crochet

The symbol crochet is another type of popular crochet and is a favorite among the Japanese. It is also known as the "chart" crochet and is another one of those crochet skills that are crucial to learn because you can make any projects from any crochet books in any language and create them all by looking at a chart.

Items made using symbol crochet:

Complicated patterns that are difficult to explain in words
Intricate designs
Motifs
Foreign language patterns

20. Tapestry Crochet

As the name goes, plenty of color goes into creating this piece, and it is also known as "intarsia" crochet. Tapestry crochet is used in many different parts of the world, and it also has many different methods which result in a variety of styles. If you want to do color work, using tapestry crochet enables you to create intricate patterns with a variety of colored yarn.

Items made using tapestry crochet:

Color workpieces
Imagery based designs

21. Tunisian Crochet

This type of crochet is done on a long hook that has a stopper at the end. When you look at Tunisian crochet, it can be very similar to knitting because of the many live loops, and you need to work your loops on and off your hook, similar to knitting.

Items made using tapestry crochet:
- Knit-look items
- Blankets
- Scarves

Chapter 4: How to Crochet for Right-Handers

Before we look at patterns, we need to study the fundamentals of crocheting which starts with how to hold a yarn. In this chapter, we will teach you not only how to crochet according to patterns, but also how to hold yarn, how to make knots and so on.

How to Hold the Yarn

One of the first things you must learn is how to hold your yarn properly. This comes before learning to secure the yarn on the crochet hook. Holding the yarn may differ depending on whether you are a right-hander or left-hander. If you are a right-hander, your left hand will be your yarn hand, and your right hand will be the one that holds the crochet hook.

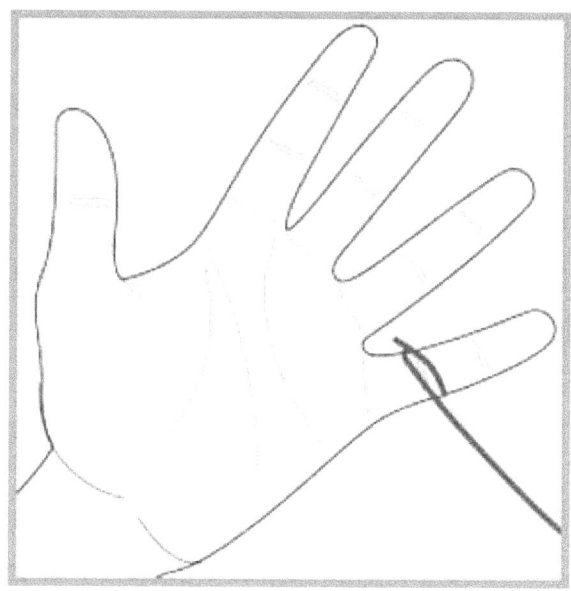

To begin, use your left hand and bring the yarn between your little finger and ring finger and wrap it just once, making a loop around the bottom little finger.

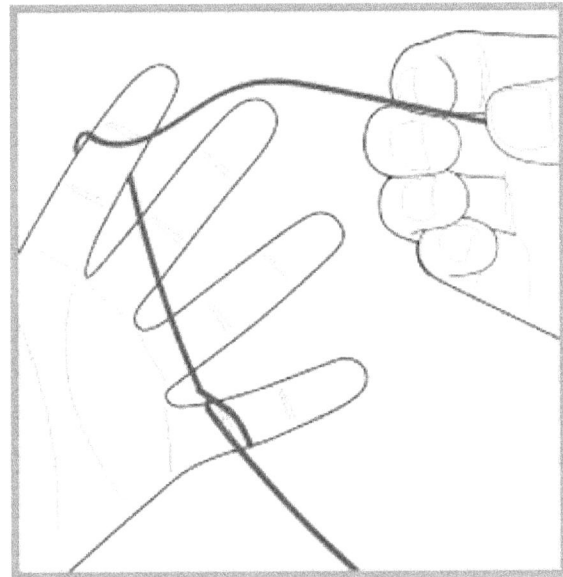

Next, move the yarn across diagonally on the inside of your hand. Then, make another loop on your ring finger by bringing it to the top of the index finger and looping it to the inside of the finger.

Next, create a slip knot. A slip knot is used to keep the yarn in place. This will give you greater control while stitching.

Firstly, lay your yarn down flat on the table. Take about six inches from the end of the yarn and create a loop that looks like a pretzel.

Next, hold the loop with your left hand and then move your crochet hook through the center of it, as seen in the image.

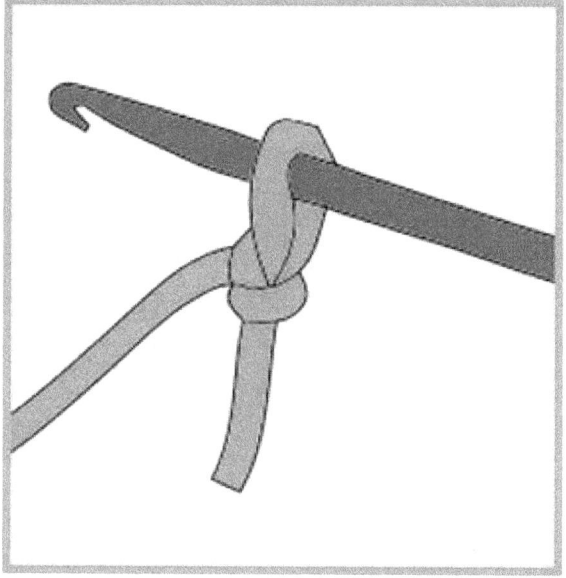

Next, tighten the loop around the hook by gently pulling both ends of the yarn. Allow a little allowance. Here, your slip knot should easily slide up and down the shaft of your hook, but it should be firm enough not come off over the end.

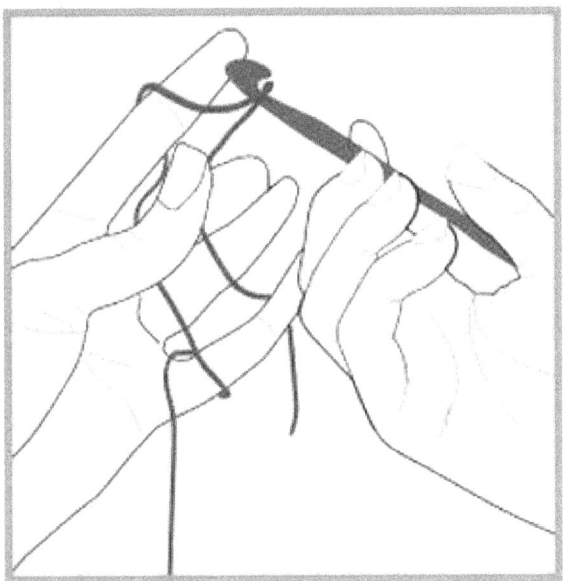

Using your middle finger and thumb to keep the yarn in place, clasp the yarn with your fingers and hold the crochet hook in your other hand. Holding your hook and yarn in this manner provides plenty of room for you to maneuver, and it also helps you control the yarn's tension by either lowering or raising your index finger.

Yarn Over

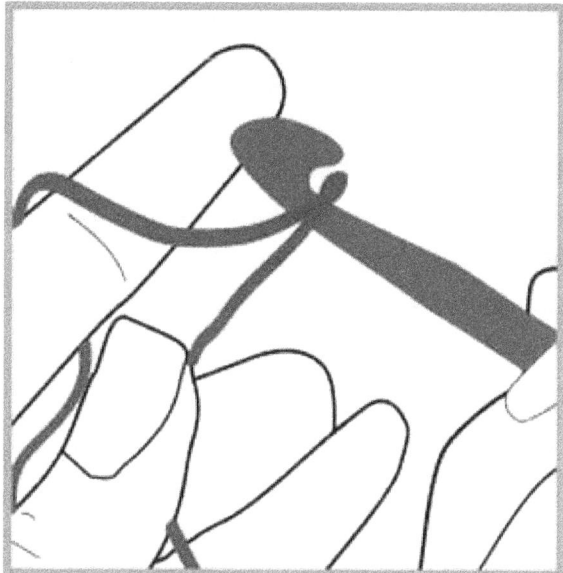

(Yo) or *yarn over* is one of the most common instructions that you will find in your crochet patterns because it is a very crucial pattern and element for each stitch. Yarn over requires you to simply loop the yarn over your hook. This process is incredibly simple. Once you are done with your slip knot, take the longer length of your yarn behind the hook and bring it over the top of the hook, then move it right into the throat to hook the yarn from the bottom.

Chain Stitch

Chain stitch or (ch) is another crucial stitch in crocheting, and it makes its appearance in just about any crochet pattern. This type of stitch is usually found at the beginning of each crochet project because it allows you to build a foundation of chain stitches which you can then build upon. The chain stitch is also known as a *joining stitch* which serves two purposes: beginning your project, and structurally connecting the previous row with the new one.

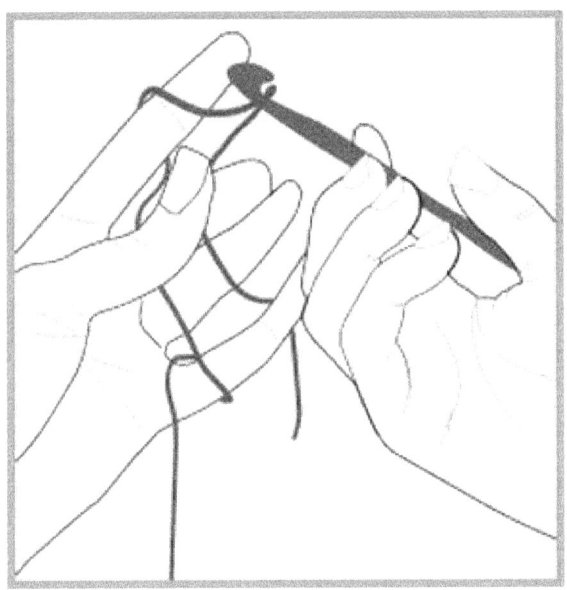

Creating the chain stitch also begins after you are done doing the slip knot. Next, hold your yarn and hook following the image above. You need to hold the tail of the slip knot between your thumb and middle finger at the same time.

Next, yarn over and then rotate the hook so that the hook faces downwards toward the slip knot.

Once done, gently tug the hook while holding the wrapped yarn, through the loop on the slip knot, and rotate the hook back upwards as you come out to the other side. This forms a chain stitch. Take note not to make the loop too tight. Don't worry if this sounds confusing. You will get the hang of it after one or two tries.

You can continue the chain stitch by repeating this process by pulling the yarn through the second loop. You need to ensure that your chain stitches are the same size so that an even tension can be procured. Once you are done completing the stitches recommended by your pattern, you have yourself a foundation chain.

How to Make a 'Magic Ring' also known as the Adjustable Loop

The stitches described above are mainly for straight patterns. It teaches you how to begin your stitching in rows. Moving forward, we will investigate designing in rounds. To begin a circular crochet pattern, learning how to make an adjustable loop is one of the easiest ways to get started. It also provides a neater finish compared to slip knots and chain stitches.

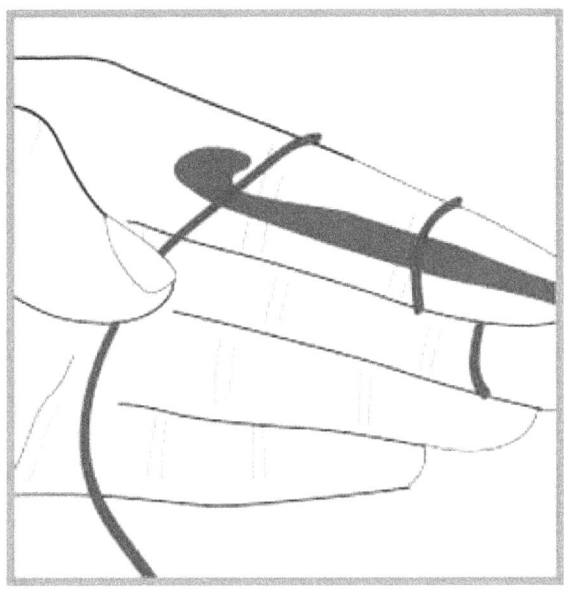

First, begin by wrapping the yarn twice around your index finger, then carefully insert the crochet hook underneath the yarn making sure to hook the second loop.

Next, pull the yarn back through the way it was inserted to create a loop.

Just like straight patterns, round patterns also require foundation chains, and this is dependent on the number of chain stitches your pattern calls for.

Create your chain stitches the way it is described above. Continue working around the loop according to the instructions on your pattern until you are done with your first round.

Gently tug at the yarn's tail to tighten the center ring so that the stitches close elegantly together.

Single Crochet Stitch

The single crochet stitch is another regular crochet stitch and is usually signified with the abbreviation (sc). This stitch is flat and tight, and it forms a compacted, finished piece, more so than other stitches. It is an extremely popular stitch used in amigurumi.

Another commonly used stitch found in crochet is the single crochet (sc) stitch. It's quite popular because of its tight and flat nature, it forms a denser finished piece compared to other stitches. Thus, it is especially popular in amigurumi!

One of the first things to do is to create a foundation chain using chain stitches. The number of stitches you need to make corresponds to the number of single crochet stitches you want your row to have including one additional chain stitch.

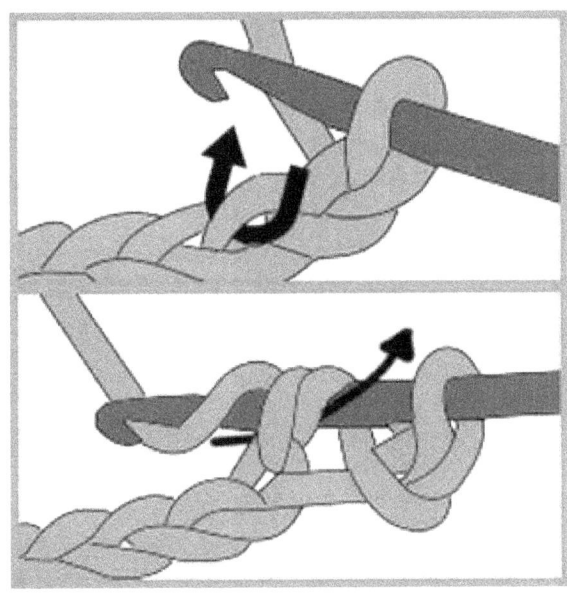

The first row of chain stitch that you make is called your *turning chain*. This means you will be using it to form a new row. Because of this, you can skip this stitch and insert your hook into the second chain stitch from the hook which would give you two loops of yarn around your crochet hook.

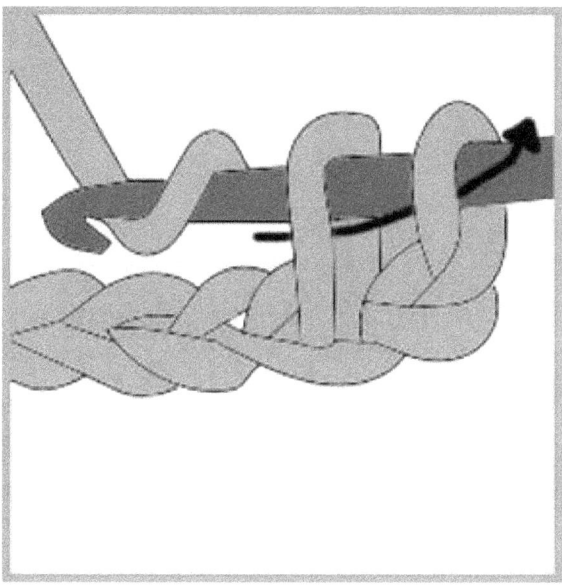

Next, yarn over and then rotate your hook's throat towards yourself and then pull it through the first loop, taking the wrapped yarn with you. You will end up with two loops around your hook.

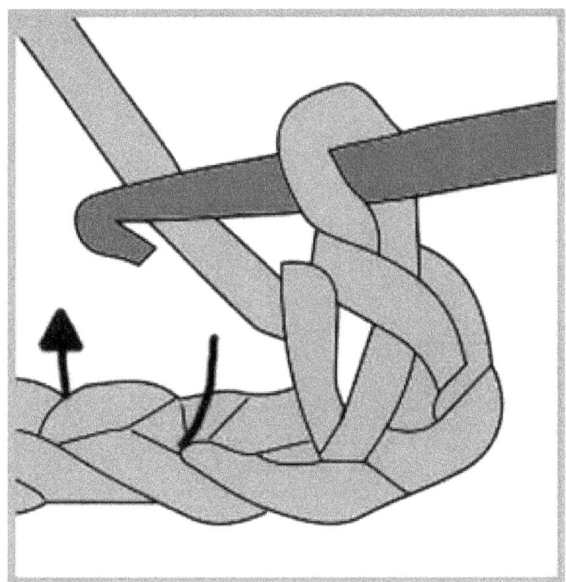

Next, yarn over again and then pull it through both loops. By now, you should only have one loop around your hook. You have now completed a single crochet stitch!

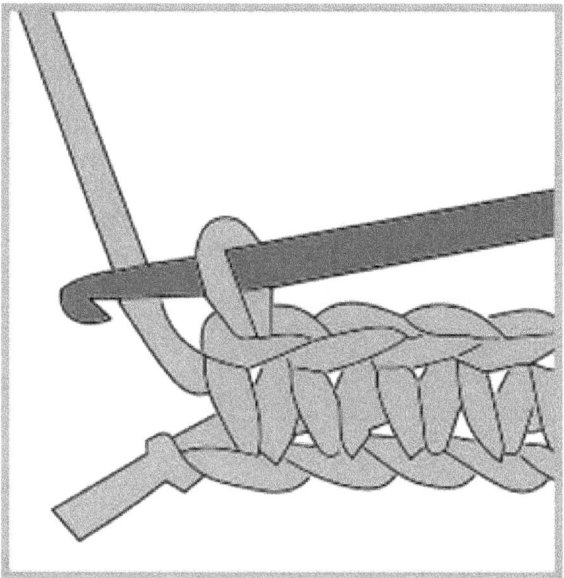

To complete a whole row of single crochet, repeat three and four in the chain stitch until you have reached the end of your row.

How to Make a Turning Chain

Firstly, congratulations on creating your first row of stitches. Now it is time to take your basic stitches to the next level. Once you are done with the first row, you will need a turning chain to add height which allows you to crochet back on your own and complete another new row. These turning chains are a combination of chain stitches, and the number of chain stitches you need to create depends on what your follow-up stitch is going to be. Follow this simple guideline:

Name of Stitch	Number of Chain Stitches
Slip Stitch (sl st)	0
Single Crochet (sc)	1
Half Double Crochet (hdc)	2
Double Crochet (dc)	3
Treble Crochet (tr)	4
Double Treble Crochet (dtr)	5

Create chain stitches in the chain stitch at the end of your first row of stitches. This will result in a turning chain.

Next, flip your crochet over so that the hook stays on the right side instead of being on the left side.

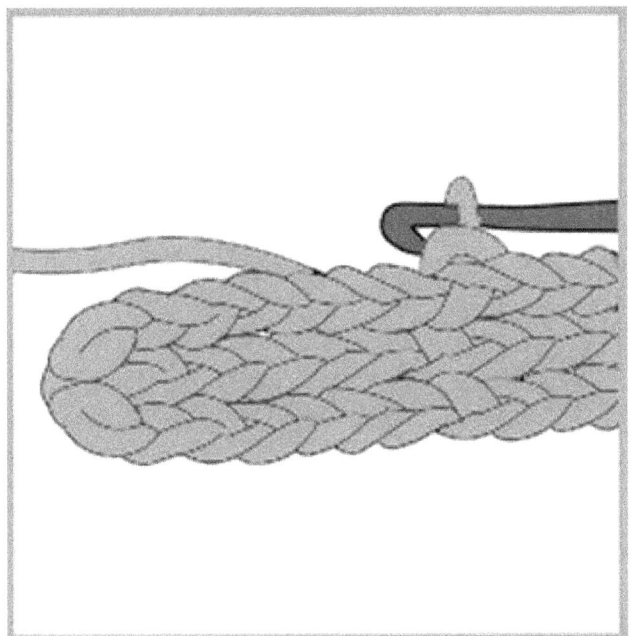

When you begin your next row, insert your crochet hook into the space next to the bottom of your turning chain. The bottom is basically the first stitch of the row. Continue stitching using the stitch that your pattern requires. Next, when you have completed another row, continue repeating the steps according to the number of rows required.

Slip Stitch

Also known as (sl st) the *slip stitch* is the flattest type of crochet stitch there is in crocheting and is chiefly used as a utility stitch to combine stitches that are used in round patterns. The best practice concerning this stitch is on the end of a foundation chain which allows you to create a ring.

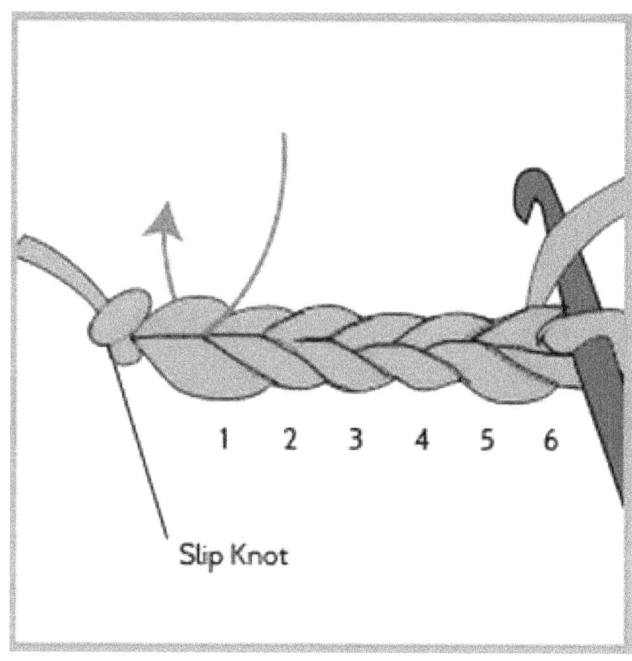

As always, begin by creating a foundation chain of six stitches and then insert the hook into your first chain stitch which forms a ring.

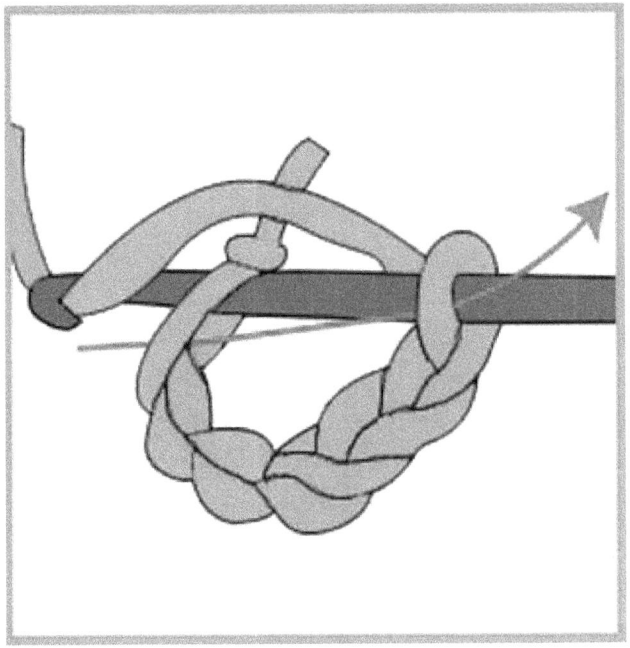

Next, yarn over and then rotate the hook's throat facing yourself. This positions the crochet hook and yarn perfectly so that you can form the slip stitch.

Next, swiftly draw the wrapped yarn back through the chain stitch and through the loop that is already on your hook. This is your first stitch slip. What you should have now is one loop left on your hook.

Half Double Crochet Stitch

(hdc) is the abbreviation for *half double crochet* and this is a relatively weird (or more complicated) stitch. It can be categorized between a single crochet and a double crochet stitch height-wise. This stitch creates a relatively tight finished result similar to a single crochet, except this stitch provides a little more give like the double crochet does.

To start off, make your foundation stitch with chain stitches amounting to seventeen. The last two stitches are reserved for your turning chain.

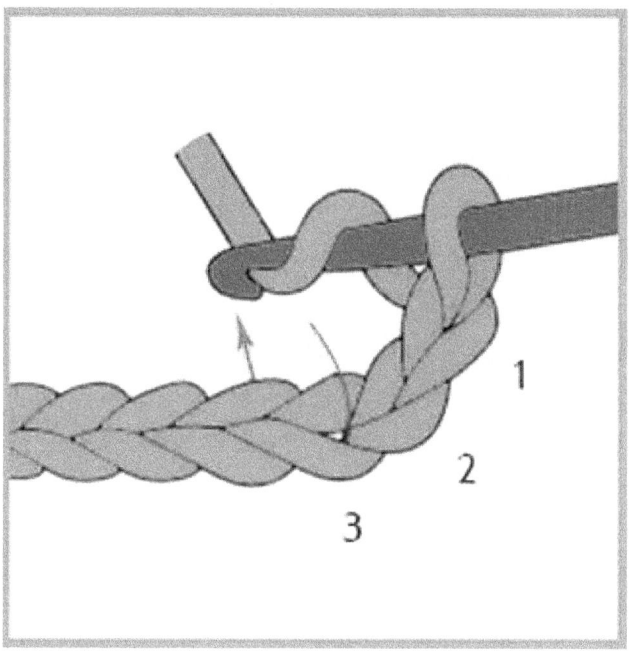

Next, yarn over and insert the hook into the third chain stitch from the hook as shown in the image.

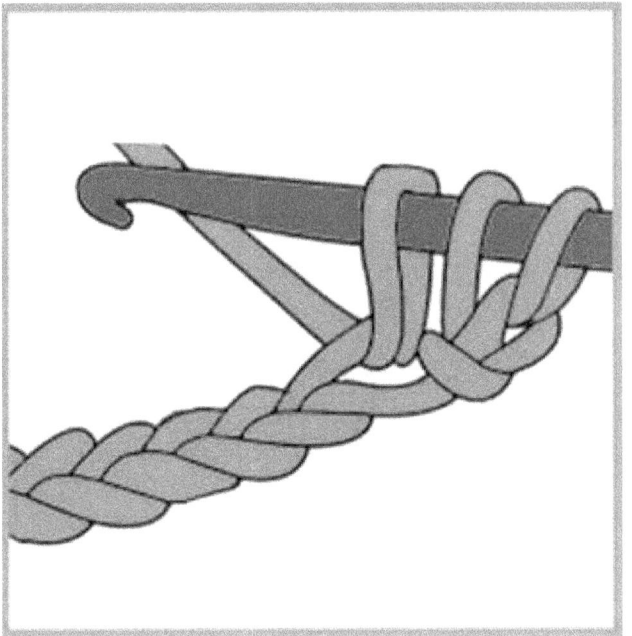

Yarn over, then gently tug at the yarn-wrapped hook back through the chain stitch. You should now have three loops around your hook.

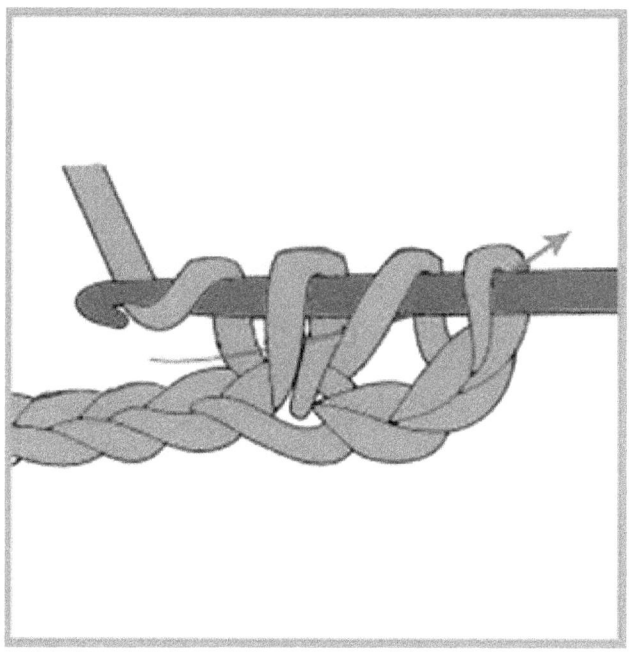

Next, yarn over again and then pull the yarn through the three loops towards your crochet hook. You have now completed your first half double crochet stitch.

To continue creating an entire row of half double crochets, all you need to do is create a half double crochet stitches each in chain stitch on your foundation row right after you have completed the first one.

Double Crochet Stitch

(dc) is the abbreviation for this type of stitch and it is another common stitch used in crochet. It measures roughly twice the height of a single crochet stitch. The resulting pattern is often solid but not too stiff and is usually used to create shawls, afghans, home accessories as well as jumpers.

Ensure your foundation chain consists of eighteen stitches, leaving the three last stitches as your turning chain.

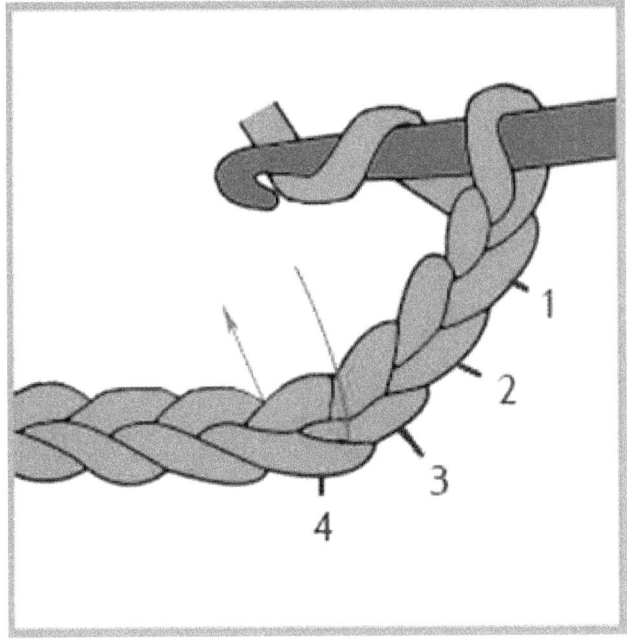

Do a yarn over and then insert your hook into the fourth chain stitch.

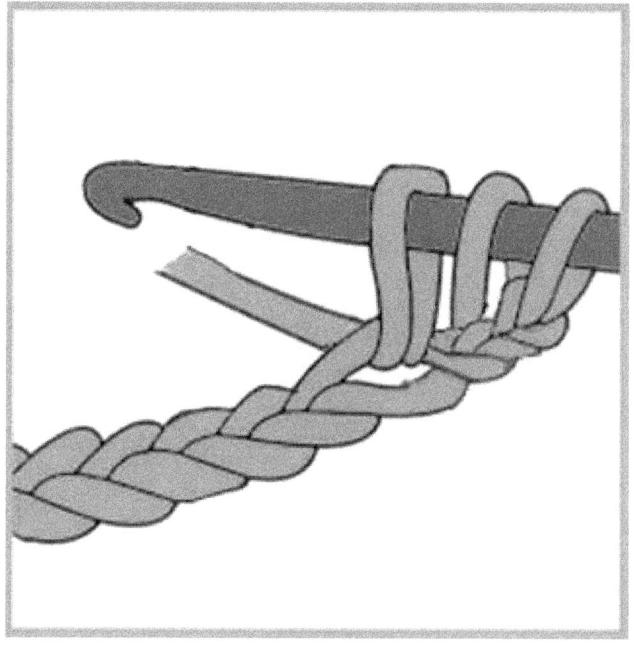

Yarn over and then pull it back gently through the chain stitch and take the wrapped yarn with you. You will now have three loops on your hook.

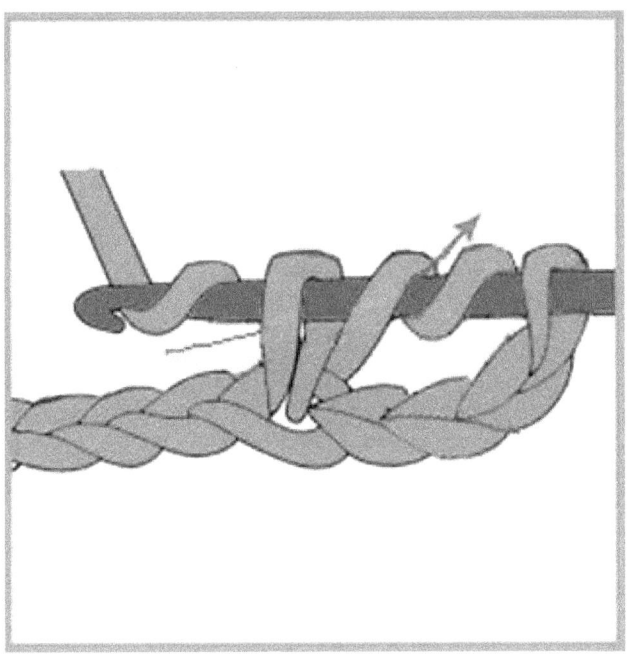

Next, yarn over and then pull the yarn through the first two loops - this will now create your double crochet stitch. You will now only have two loops around your hook.

Yarn over again and then gently pull the wrapped yarn again through the remaining two loops. This will result in completing your first ever double crochet stitch. You will only have one loop left on your crochet hook.

To complete an entire row of double crochet, you can start by making a double crochet stitch in every chain stitch on your foundation row.

Treble Crochet Stitch

(tr) is the abbreviation for *treble crochet* or *triple crochet* and it results in loose stitches that are slightly taller than the double crochet stitches. It is ideal for larger garments as well as home accessories.

Start by creating a nineteen-chain stitch foundation stitch, leaving the last four stitches for your turning chain.

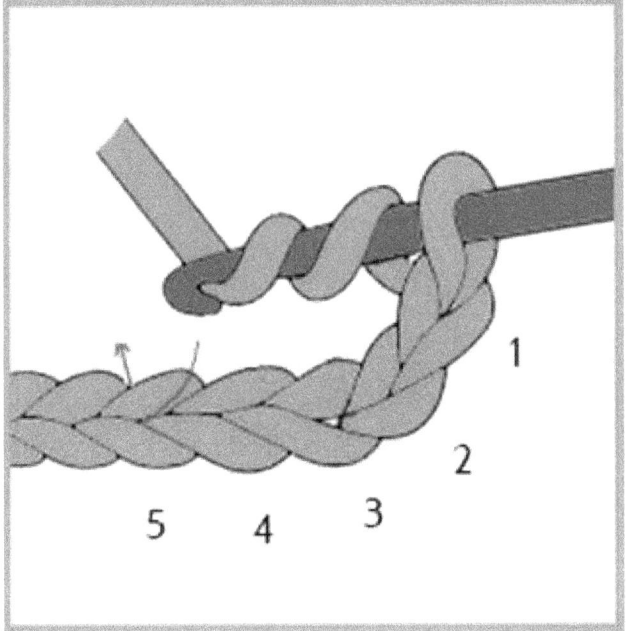

Do a yarn over two times and then include your crochet hook directly into the fifth chain stitch from the hook.

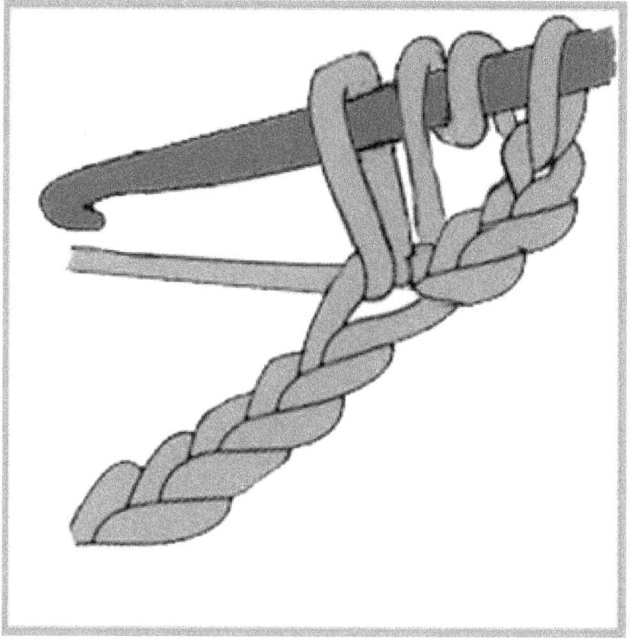

Yarn over again and then gently pull the wrapped crochet hook back through the chain stitch. You now have all four loops on your hook.

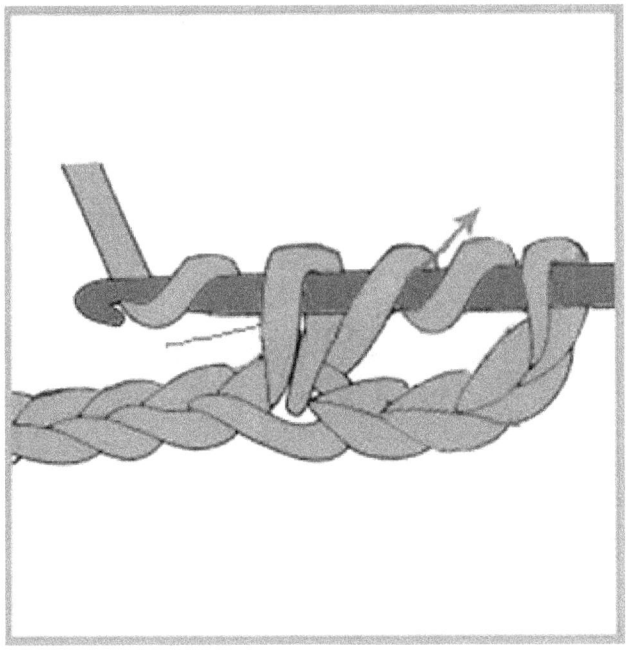

Yarn over and then tug the yarn back through the first two loops on your hook.

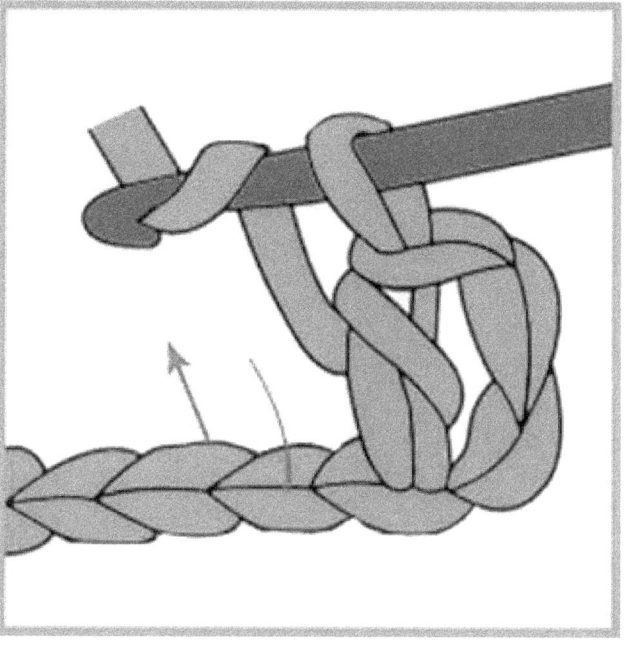

Yarn over again and then pull the yarn back through the consecutively two loops on your hook.

Yarn over again and then pull the yarn back through the last two loops on your hook. Now you have completed your first treble crochet stitch with only one loop left on your crochet hook.

To complete the entire row of treble crochet, you need to yarn over twice and then insert your crochet hook into the next chain along your foundation chain.

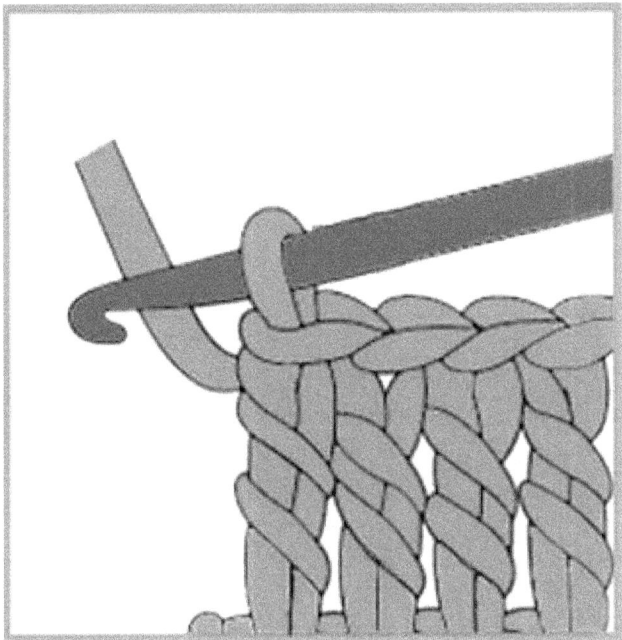

Continue to create treble crochet stitches in each available chain stitch across the foundation chain until you have a complete row.

How to Fasten Off Your Yarn

Learning to fasten the end of your project is essential in any form of needlecraft. Just like in crocheting, you would also need to fasten your yarn at the end of your crochet piece so that it stays secure and in place, preventing your stitches from unraveling.

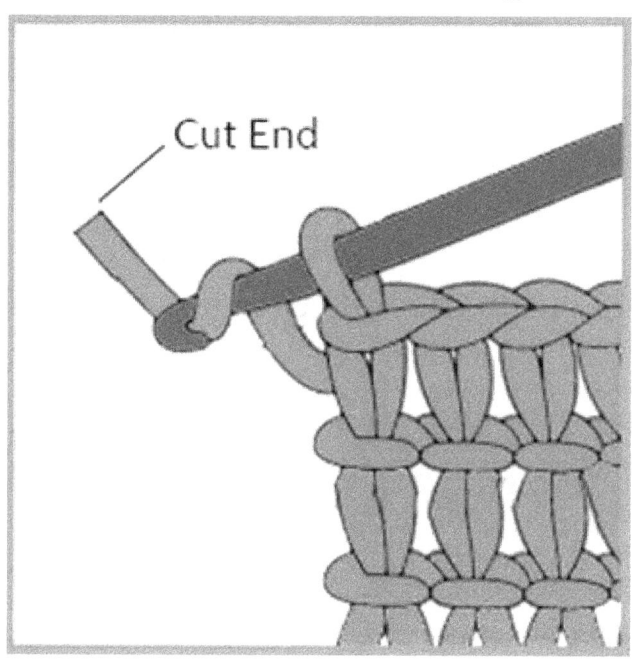

Cut your yarn and leave at least six inches of yarn from the hook. Next, pull the loose end through the final remaining loop on your hook. Remove the hook and tug gently on the yarn's tail to tighten the tail end.

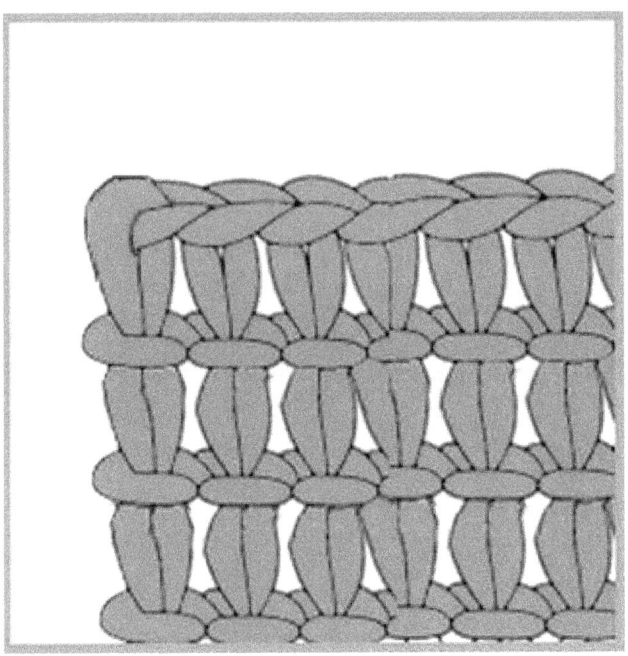

Take a yarn needle and weave the yarn tail through two, three, or even four crochet stitches in your pattern to hide it.

Now you have yourself a final product with a perfectly neat finish!

Chapter 5: How to Crochet for Left-Handers

Don't worry, we've got left-handed crocheters covered in this book too. Back in the day, left-handed crocheters had to learn the craft 'backwards' because they learned the craft from right-handed crocheters. But now, there is no need to do that any longer. There are plenty of tutorials, teachers and patterns for left-handed crocheters.

Basic Understanding of Left-Handed Crochet

Left-handed crochet is practically a mirror image of right-handed crochet. For left-handed crocheters, you would need to hold the crochet hook in your left hand and the yarn in the right hand. You can either use a knife grip or a pencil grip to hold the hook and manipulate the yarn the way a right-handed crocheter would do. While you can follow the instructions from your teacher or from tutorials, you can also decide what is comfortable for you.

While most of the crochet tutorials are written for right-handers, left-handers can follow the exact same instructions but in the opposite direction. This also means that when left-handers work in rows, the first row will be worked into the foundation chain beginning from the left side and ending at the right. As a left-hander, this is natural. When working with rounds, you will be crocheting clockwise compared to right-handers who will work counter-clockwise.

How to Crochet Chain Left-Handed

In this chapter, we will learn to crochet the three most basic crochet stitches which include the chain, single crochet, and double crochet, all using the left hand. More types of stitches can be learned online using various tutorials and videos.

1. Start with a slip knot.

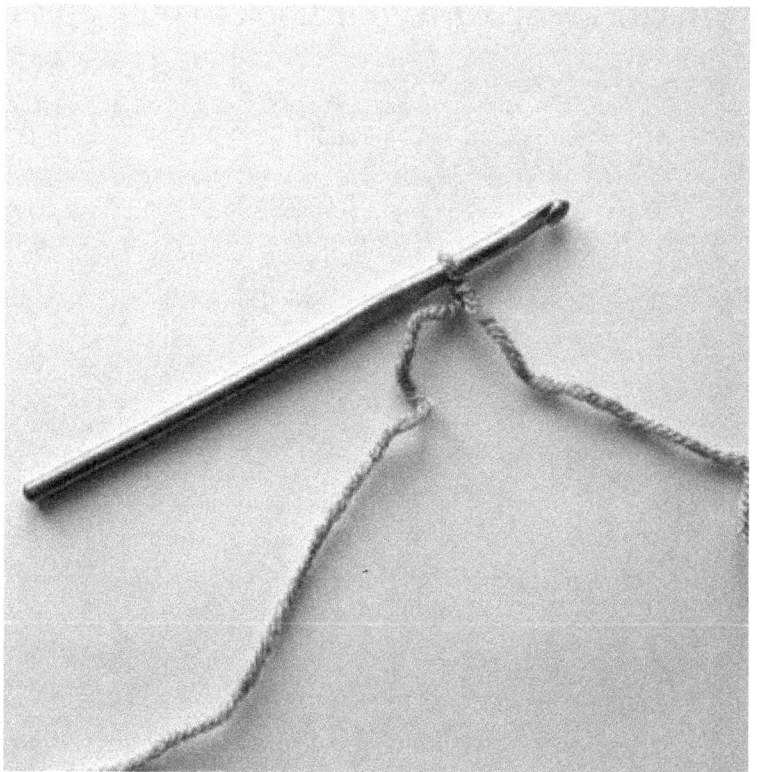

2. As usual, start with your yarn over. Each time you yarn over, you are scooping the yarn clockwise with your hook to pick up the yarn.

2. Draw your hook through the loop. Here you will loop the yarn clockwise.

From here on, repeat steps one, two, and three. Take note that each repetition is one chain.

How to Single Crochet Left-Handed

1. Begin by crocheting a foundation chain with the length of your choice.

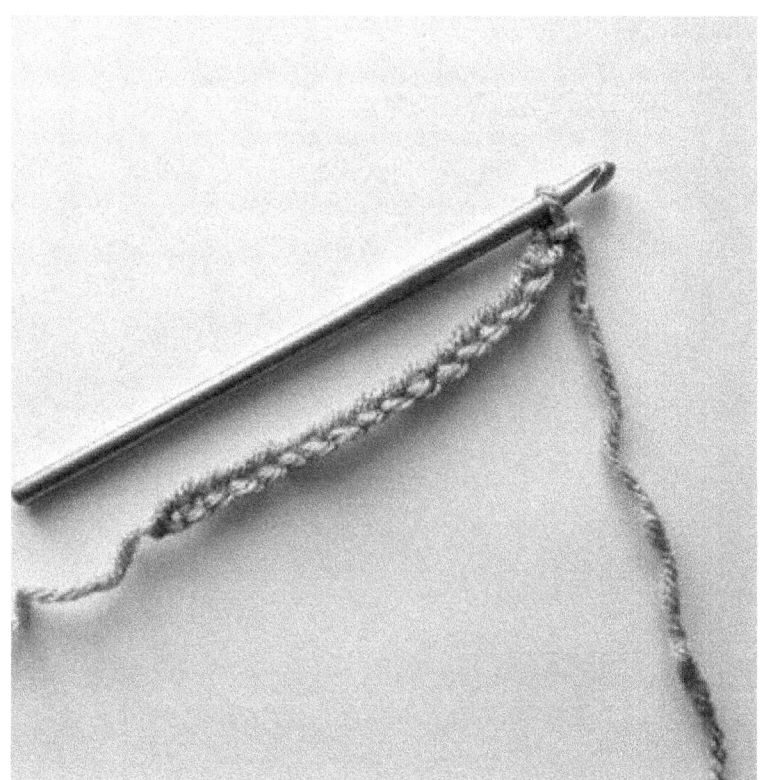

2. Now, insert your hook into the second chain that is to the right of the hook. Always make sure your hook is in your left hand, and the chain extends out to the right hand.

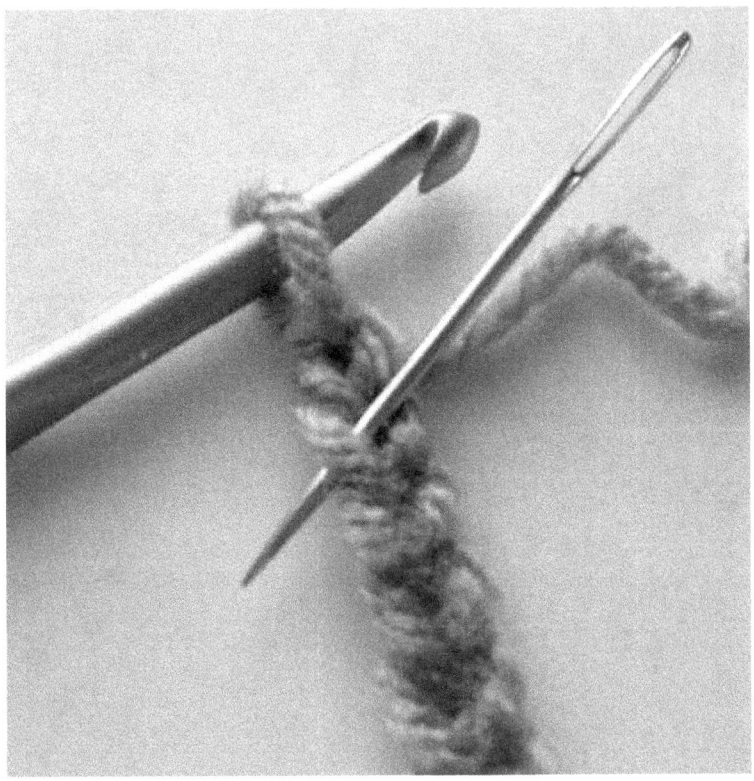

3. In the image above, it shows how you will get into the chain using your hook, and you also have two loops on top of the hook and one below. Yarn over.

4. Next, draw a loop through, and now you will see two loops on your hook at the end of this step.

5. Yarn over again.

6. When you are at this step, pull your hook through both loops. Now you have made your very first (sc) or single crochet. Well done!

7. Now all you need to do is insert your hook into the very next chain and repeat steps three through six. Thereafter, repeat step seven across the row.

How to Double Crochet Left-Handed

1. To start this, you need to create a set of foundation chains according to the length of your choice, or according to the pattern. These are the same steps a right-handed crocheter would follow.

2 Yarn over.

3. Now, insert your hook into the fourth chain which is located towards the right, because you are working from the left of your hook.

4. Now, yarn over again.

5. In this step, you need to draw your hook through the loop. Here, you will notice three loops on your hook when you reach the end of the step.

6. Now yarn over and then draw your hook through the first two of those three loops on the hook.

7. Next, yarn over again and here, you need and draw your hook through the two loops. Congratulations, you have now completed your first ever double crochet as a left-handed!

To continue your double crochet, begin with doing a yarn over and then insert the hook into the next stitch. You should repeat steps four to seven, followed by repeating step eight across row.

From here on, yarn over and insert your crochet hook into the next stitch.

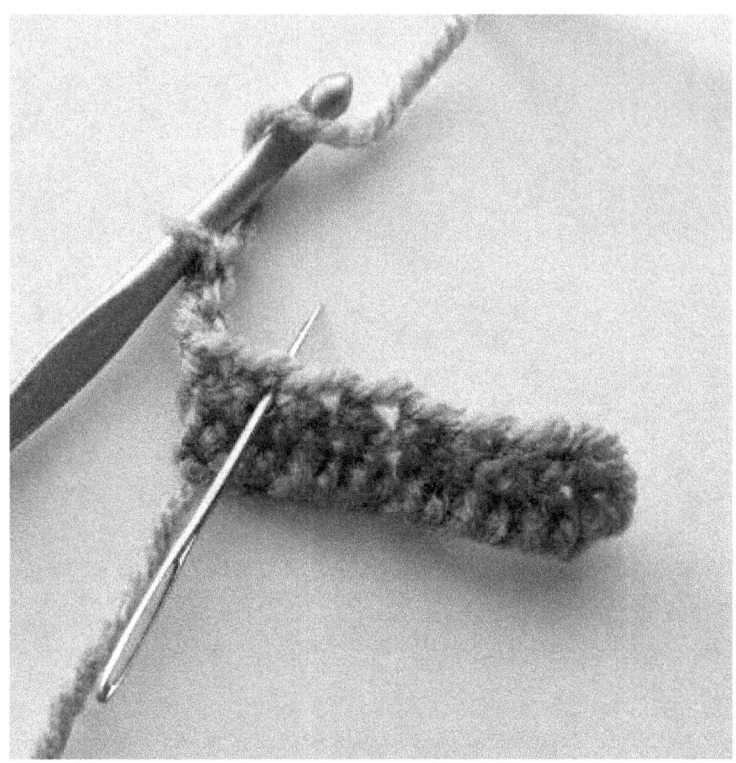

If you observe the photo above, it shows that you are starting your next stitch into the third chain of the turning chain from the row before. This is done to ensure that the stitch count remains correct and the shape is not triangular. Next, all you need to do is repeat your (dc) stitches across the entire row.

Tips for Left-Handed Crochet

- When you leave your beginning yarn tail hanging at the beginning of each project, do not crochet over the tail.
- When a pattern mentions either the right side or the wrong side, look for the tail as a cue. The right side will always be where the tail is on the bottom right corner.
- Each time you yarn over, simple scoop the yarn clockwise. This is especially crucial when you are a beginner. Both written and visual patterns can be achieved using left-handed crocheters. You can always reverse images with charts and graphs. Once you have reversed the image, you may use it as a guide.

How to Adapt Patterns to Left-Handed Crochet

Rest assured if you think there aren't enough left-handed crochet patterns, we have a simple solution for you. Just about any straightforward crochet pattern can be followed the way it is written. All left-handed crocheters need to do is reverse the direction that they are working in.

However, some patterns need to be reversed properly so that they work the same way they do in their original form. In tapestry crochet for example and most crochets that require colorwork, you will need to reverse the pattern.

Otherwise, you will end up with a reversed image that looks backwards. For instance, words could end up spelled backwards.

If a right-handed crocheter worked the pattern with odd rows from right to left, the left-handed crocheter would need to work on them from right to left.

Most symbol charts are written for right-handers, so if you are using a symbol chart, use the same number of stitches but work in the opposite direction. You just need to mirror the chart.

Some people can reverse this pattern in their head, but this takes time and requires experience. It's okay if you cannot do this. All you need to do is create a mirror image of the pattern for yourself, so technically, you can use any graph, symbol, or chart and reverse it. You can do this by using photo editing tools that will automatically reverse the instructions. You can also do this by using an actual mirror to reverse the image.

For written patterns, go through the pattern instructions and highlight the cues indicating the direction to work towards. If you see instructions such as, "connect yarn to right corner," or "work into the wrong side of the work," this would mean that you need to reverse the instruction in your head or write your notes on it, so you don't forget. So, your instructions would be joining the yarn to the left corner or working on the right side of the project.

Chapter 6: Tips and Tricks to Crocheting

Every crocheter requires tips and tricks to become a pro. These tips and tricks help make things easier when you begin crocheting.

Crocheting Using Thread

When it comes to crocheting thread, remember that smaller is bigger. Threads are labeled according to their thickness. The thicker the thread, the smaller is the number. It is counterintuitive, but the more you crochet, the more you will get used to it.

- As a beginner, you can always start with a crochet thread three, then move up to a five and ten. Size twenty or thirty threads can be used once you have built up your skills.

- As with the crochet threads, follow the same approach with steel crochet hooks. The smaller the size, the bigger the crochet hook. You can also look at the mm size that is usually printed on the hook itself. For example, a hook sized nine is 1.25 mm while the hook sized ten is 1.15 mm.

- As a beginner, you should start with a hook size that the pattern calls for. Once you have honed your skills a little more, you can adjust your hooks based on your comfort level and gauge.

- For beginners, it is always good to use steel crochet hooks. These hooks are much easier to use when it comes to working with thread.

- People often find crocheting using thread more difficult compared to using yarn, and it is only because of the thinner hooks involved. When you are working with the thread, all you need to do is choose a hook that has a bigger handle - that's all!

- When purchasing thread, always buy a crochet thread and steer clear from embroidery or sewing thread. Although you can crochet with almost anything that resembles yarn or thread, you can make your life easier by sticking to the kind of thread that is meant for crocheting.

- When you work with yarn overs, make sure to work closely with the crochet hook head. You always want to ensure that the work on the hook is done above the section of the hook where it starts to get wider.

Otherwise, your loops will be extremely loose.

- Another tip would be to thread around your non-crocheting hand, so it is easier to control your tension. This is extremely helpful when thread crocheting.

Crocheting Hacks with Yarn

- To prevent the balls of yarn from falling and rolling away while you are crocheting, put them in a hand wipe container. Just make sure to wash and clean it first. The yarn can be pulled through the hole of the hand wipe container.

- Use bobby pins or safety pins, or even a paper clip to mark your rows, or stitch a colored yarn or thread into the valley of the first stitch. Bobby pins and paper clips can be pulled out later once you are done.

- Use pencil boxes or jewelry boxes, or even a toothbrush holder to store your hooks. Food containers and snack containers can also do the trick.

- Using *Excel* sheets to map out your patterns. This is a great way to keep track of where you left off when your crocheting gets interrupted. You can also make the pattern larger to decrease eye strain.

- To figure out the amount of yarn or thread needed for a certain project, calculate the number of rows you can get out of one skein/ball, then determine how many rows your project requires. Then, divide the number of rows the project requires with the number of rows your ball gives you. You will be able to calculate how much yarn is needed this way.

- If you are worried about purchasing too much colored yarn that you won't be using in the future, just buy white washable yarn and dye it according to the pattern's colors.

- To keep your project in place, use yarn needles instead of hooks to weave the ends back through. This holds the project better and eliminates the chances of the yarn traveling.

- Dip the end of the yarn in clear nail polish to make it go through the eye of a needle. When you dip it, twist the yarn tight while it dries.

- Instead of ironing your projects, which is not always ideal, mix water and starch in equal parts and spray liberally on your project. Leave to dry on a flat surface.

- To store patterns in a three-ring notebook, use sheet protectors.
- Keeping an index card with the lists of hooks and yarns you have is a great way to keep inventory. This ensures that the next time you are short of crochet supplies, you already know what you need.
- Yarns and other unfinished projects can be kept in zipper bags.
- It is always a good idea to keep foldable sewing scissors so that they don't snag in your crocheting bag.
- When in doubt, sew more tightly with string than you would with yarn. Try not to stitch so firmly that you hurt your hands. Knit somewhat more firmly than normal (except if you're now a skilled crocheter, at that point, simply do what you generally do!).
- Pay attention to the steps you're about to follow before you figure with thread crochet. Jumping from an okay hook size, labored with a cumbersome yarn all the way down to thread crochet can make your thread paintings appear unbearably tiny. Steadily work your way down to the smaller sizes.
- Always do your crochet work in good light so that you don't strain your eyes. This also makes crocheting easier. This is the same reason why, as beginners, you need to work with a lighter colored thread as it makes it easier for you to find those little stitches.
- Crocheting is fun! Sure, it does have its own challenges, but that's only something you'll need to overcome at the beginning. Learning takes time, so be patient with yourself and enjoy each project you work on.
- Always choose beginner patterns when you're starting off. This will make it easier for you to learn how to combine stitches and learn the ropes of crocheting.
- Working with a simple crochet swatch that uses basic stitches is always ideal, simply to get the best results, minus the pressure of going through with a pattern.

Chapter 7:
Choosing a Crochet Pattern

For beginners, you want to choose a crochet pattern that is easy, but also one that's fun to work with. Once you are comfortable with your skills, you can upgrade to more advanced patterns. As a beginner, you want to take baby steps and enjoy the crocheting process instead of becoming overwhelmed with an advanced pattern and get discouraged. This might cause you to give up on your crocheting journey altogether. There are plenty of beautiful crochet patterns to try for beginners. One way to identify what would work best for you is to look at the crochet pattern schematic.

Understanding the Crochet Pattern

When you have chosen a pattern, the next thing to do is to read the instructions entirely, which also includes the stitch guide, any notes that come with it, the diagrams, charts, and the finishing sections. Confusion can be avoided by reading these notes. You will also find plenty of information on tips and techniques, construction, guidelines for keeping track of your stitches, as well as what to do with scrap yarn. As a beginner, you will seek immense knowledge by going through the stitch guide and identifying the kinds of stitches that you have never tried before.

Gauge Swatch

The gauge swatch is very important for beginners, although it is often considered the least interesting part of crocheting. Despite its unpopular reputation, the gauge swatch will help you determine the size of your final product.

The gauge swatch is important, especially if you are substituting yarn with all yarns having the same size or weight. When you use substituted yarn, along with the individual crochet tension that goes with it, you may not always end up with the exact gauge with your hook size. If you end up with a wrong or different gauge size, try using a smaller or larger hook depending on your project. This tiny step can make a huge difference to your overall project.

Substituting Yarn in Crochet Patterns

When you do decide to substitute the yarn specified in your pattern, you would need to look for the correct yarn size. If your pattern calls for worsted weight yarn, then look for another type of worsted weight yarn. This does not mean that your yarn size will be correct, but it may require you to play around with different hook sizes to get the right gauge.

Wraps per inch are the best indicator of correct yarn size substitute. *Wraps per inch* or (wpi), can be found by wrapping the yarn continuously around a ruler and then counting the number of wraps you can make in an inch. Keep the fiber content in mind when you substitute yarn. Silk and cotton often have a different drape compared to animal fiber such as wool or alpaca. Pure silk and cotton also have a stretch, and it can 'grow' over time. You can also use acrylic blends or even acrylic yarn as alternatives to animal or plant fibers.

A final note to any beginner is to always believe in your pattern. Anyone attempting this for the first time is bound to hit a number of road bumps and dead ends, and it is the same for you and your crocheting. Even designers are always pushing the envelope and discovering new techniques for stitch textures and unique constructions, so this should not discourage you from completing an easy crocheting pattern that you love. Sometimes, the most confusing sections of a crochet pattern for both beginners and even advanced crocheters is understanding the pattern, but as you work on them, it will become much clearer.

It may sound a bit overwhelming, but once you have a firm understanding of how to read crochet patterns, everything will become a lot easier. Always start with something that is easier to understand and meant for beginners.

Chapter 8:
Easy and Fun Crochet Patterns for Beginners

As a beginner, finding easy and fun patterns for your first few projects are crucial for starting your crochet journey. This will help you get the hang of reading patterns, improve hand-eye coordination between the yarn, the hook and the stitches, and most importantly, it will allow you to build enough confidence to get through the entire project. Once you have finished it, you may move on to more advanced patterns in due time. Whether you are crocheting as a hobby, or wish to make Christmas gifts for everybody, the patterns described in this section are great for beginners and are an excellent way to kickstart your crocheting journey.

Small Things

1. Simple Bow

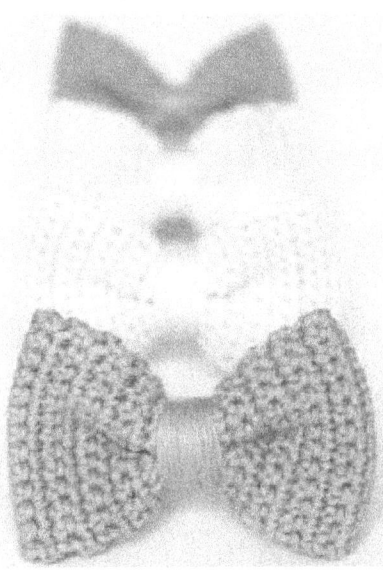

Are you itching to start a quick and easy project? Are you looking for useful crochet projects that will make use of those scrap yarns? I've got you covered! The next few pages are filled with small projects like a coin purse, a bow, motifs, and more.

This project will surely add character and a personalized touch to any hair tie, headband, a shirt, a beanie, a denim jacket, or on a present.

Note: *This works well with any kind of yarn, just make sure you use the appropriate hook according to the yarn's thickness.*

1st Row

1. Make 12 Chains.

2nd to 22nd Row

1. Make 12 DCs on top of the previous row.

How to Assemble

1. Sew both the 1st and 22nd rows together.
2. Lay it flat with the seam in the middle.
3. Pinch the middle with your thumb and index finger and loop the remaining yarn around the strip to form a bow.

4. Secure the yarn at the pack of the bow, fasten in place, and tuck off the ends.

2. Crochet Scrunchie

This lovely, personalized scrunchie will be a great gift for your female friends and family members.

Note: *This works well with any kind of yarn, just make sure you use the appropriate hook according to the yarn's thickness. Here, I suggest a light cotton 3-ply thread.*

1st Round

1. Make a slip knot into the ponytail band. Work your 1st SC.
2. Make 3 Chains, then SC into the band.
3. Repeat step 2 until you've covered the entire band. Allow them to overlap each other to hide the band completely.
4. When completely covered, Slip stitch into your 1st stitch.

2nd Row

1. SC into the 1st Chain Space you come across.
2. Chain 3 and SC into the Chain Space of 3.

3. Repeat step 2 until you've gone through each Chain Space of 3.

4. Slip stitch into your 1st stitch.

3rd Round

1. Slipstitch into the nearest Chain Space and make Chain 3. Make 5 DCs into the same Chain Space, then SC into the next Chain Space.

2. Make 6 DCs into the next Chain Space, and then 1 SC into the next Chain Space.

3. Repeat step 2 until you've reached your 1st stitch for this round. Fasten it off and tuck in ends.

3. Rainbow Fold-Over Coin Purse

Easy, simple, and eye catching—talk about aesthetical and functional. Have fun making this in rainbow shades, gradient shades, or alternate between your favorite colors.

Note: *This works well with any kind of yarn, just make sure you use the appropriate hook according to the yarn's thickness.*

1st Round

1. Make a Magic Ring.
2. Make 3 Chains and 12 DCs into the Magic Ring.
3. Slip stitch into the 1st stitch you made and fasten off. You should have 13 stitches in total.

2nd Round

Change yarn color.

1. Make a DC into one of the stitches from the previous row. Pass in a 2nd DC into the same stitch.
2. Finish this round by making 2 DCs in each stitch from the previous round.
3. Slip stitch into the 1st stitch you made and fasten off. You should have 26 DCs in total.

3rd Round

Change yarn color.

1. Start with 1 DC into any stitch from the previous round.
2. In the next stitch, make 2 DCs into the same stitch, and make 1

DC in the next stitch.

3. Repeat step 2 until you finish this round, alternating between 2 DCs and 1 DC.

4. Slip stitch into your 1st stitch and fasten off. You should have 39 DCs.

4th Round

Change yarn color.

1. Make two DCs in two separate stitches.

2. Make 2 DCs into one stitch.

3. Repeat steps 1 and 2 until you finish this round, alternating between 2 DCs in two separate stitches and one 2 DCs in the same stitch.

4. Slip stitch into the 1st stitch you made and fasten off. You should have 52 DCs.

5th Round

Change yarn color.

1. In this round, make 3 DCs in three separate stitches, and stitch in 2 DCs into the 4th stitch.

2. Keep alternating between 3 DCs in three separate stitches, and stitch in 2 DCs into the 4th stitch

3. Slipstitch into the first stitch you made and fasten off. You should have 65 DCs.

6th Round

Change yarn color.

1. In this round, make 4 DCs in three separate stitches, and stitch in 2 DCs into the 5th stitch.

2. Keep alternating between 4 DCs in three separate stitches, and stitch in 2 DCs into the 5th stitch

3. Slipstitch into the first stitch you made and fasten off. You should have 78 DCs.

7th Round

Change yarn color.

1. In this round, make 5 DCs in three separate stitches, and stitch in 2 DCs into the 6th stitch.
2. Keep alternating between 5 DCs in three separate stitches, and stitch in 2 DCs into the 6th stitch
3. Slipstitch into the first stitch you made and fasten off. You should have 91 DCs.

How to Assemble

1. With a needle and thread, sew in a zipper on half of the circle.
2. Fold over, and sew in the other half onto the other side of the zipper.
3. Embellish with beads and sequins or leave as is.

4. Tube Pencil Case

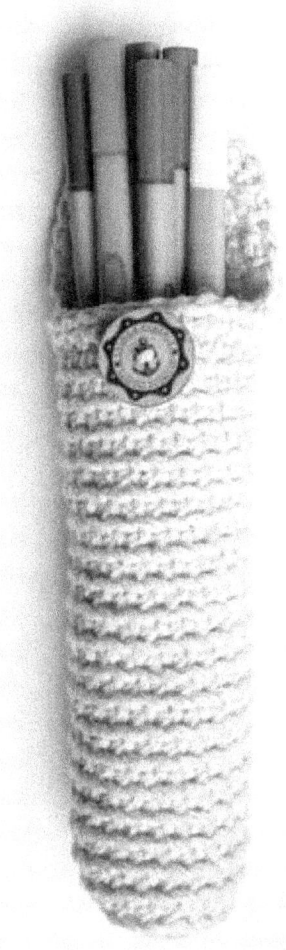

We all could use a cute pencil case! Try making this convenient and easy-to-fashion pencil case for yourself or a loved one.

Note: *This works well with any kind of yarn, just make sure you use the appropriate hook according to the yarn's thickness.*

You will need

- Needle
- Button

We will be working around this project in a spiral, so no need to make a slip stitch after every round.

1st Round

1. Make a Magic Ring.

2. Make 6 SCs into the Magic Ring.

2nd Round

1. Make 2 SCs in each stitch from the previous round. You should have 12 SCs in total.

3rd Round

1. Make 2 SCs in one stitch, then follow up with 2 SCs in two stitches.
2. Repeat step 1 until you finish this round. You should have a total of 18 SCs.

4th Round

1. SC the back loop only of each stitch from the previous round, maintaining 18 SCs throughout each round. Repeat this step until you get to your desired length.

Closure Flap

1st Row

1. Chain 1 and then turn your work over.
2. Make 7 SCs

2nd to 5th Row

1. Repeat 1st row.

6th Row

1. Chain 1 then turn your work over.
2. Make 2 SCs into the next 2 stitches, then Chain 3, skip 3 stitches, and finally SC into the last 2 stitches.

7th Row

1. Make 1 Chain and SC through all 7 stitches from the previous row.
2. Now slowly keep making SCs around the flap and the rim of the pencil case to make it look neat. Slip stitch, fasten off, and tuck in the ends.

Position the button and sew in place. Fasten off and tuck in the ends.

5. African Flower Hexagon

This is one of the most versatile patches you will find in the history of crochet. If you join them together, you can create unique things like stuffed animals, blankets, pillowcases, balls, purses, and so much more. The trick to it is to use random colors to make it brighter and eye catching. This is a good way to make use of scrap yarns.

The pattern is pretty straightforward and easy to do. Connecting it together and experimenting with ideas is what will creativity and style.

Note: *This works well with any kind of yarn, just make sure you use the appropriate hook according to the yarn's thickness.*

1st Row

1. Start with a Magic Ring.
2. Chain 3 (this will be considered as your 1st DC) and next to it, make a DC, and then a Chain.
3. Make five more sets of 2 DCs and one Chain stitch. You will end up with 6 in total.
4. After your last Chain, slip stitch into your first DC (the 3 Chains).

2nd Row

This will be a good time to change colors.

1. Fasten off into the first Chain to your left.
2. This row will consist of Chain-centered fan stitches. Having said that, Chain 3, DC into the Chain Space, Chain 1, 2 DCs into the same Chain Space. Continue until you have 6 of these around

your circle. One set for each Chain from the previous row.

3. End this row by slip stitching into your first stitch.

3rd Row

1. Fasten off into the first Chain to your left.

2. Now create a full fan of 7 DCs. 1st fan should consist of 3 Chain and 6 DCs. Make 6 of these, 1 set for each Chain from the previous row.

3. And like before, end this row with a slip stitch to your first stitch.

4th Row

This will be a good time to change colors again.

1. This row will consist of SCs. Fasten off into the second DC from the previous row.

2. Start making your SCs around the previous row's DCs.

3. When you reach where the fans of the previous row meet, make a long stitch, going through all the way to where the fans from the 2nd row meet.

4. Continue your SCs around the fans, do not forget to make a long stitch where the fans meet.

5. When you've gone all around the flower, slip stitch into your 1st stitch.

5th Row

This is another time to change colors if you please.

1. Make SCs around the flower again, but this time, only in the back loops.

2. Take off from your last stitch you had left off, make 3 SCs, and when you reach the "corner" of the hexagon (which is the 4th stitch from the previous row, in other words, the center of the "petal"), make a Chain before making another SC in the same stitch.

3. Keep making SCs on the back loops of the previous row,

remembering that when you reach the center stitch of the "petal" you need to make a Chain, and then make a SC again in the same loop the last stitch was in.

6. African Flower Pin Cushion

Are you tired of that old tomato pin cushion? Make your sewing kit bright and cheerful with this lovely project.

Note: *This works well with any kind of yarn, just make sure you use the appropriate hook according to the yarn's thickness.*

How to Assemble

1. Make two African Flower Hexagons (*pattern in this* book).
2. Sew on buttons in the center of both African Flower Hexagons.
3. SC both their edges together. Just before you're about to close the seam, stuff it with polyester filling to make it puff up.
4. Continue your SC until it's fully closed.
5. Slip stitch into your 1st stitch.
6. Fasten off and tuck the ends away.

7. Classic Granny Square

Whether you're a newbie or a pro, every crocheter must know this pattern! This motif is as versatile as the African Flower Hexagon, but this one is a go-to patch for making basic yet beautiful afghans.

Note: *This works well with any kind of yarn, just make sure you use the appropriate hook according to the yarn's thickness.*

<u>It is important to check tension and maintain even stitches.</u>

1st Row

1. Start with a Magic Ring.
2. Chain 3 and make 2 DC in the Magic Ring.
3. Chain 2, and make 3 DC in the Magic Ring. Repeat 2 more times until you have 4 sets, forming a roundish square.
4. Slip stitch into your 1st stitch. You should have 12 DC stitches in total.

2nd Row

1. Turn your work over and in the Chain Space you made in 1st row, Chain 3, then make 2 DCs.
2. Chain 2 and make 3 DCs in the same Chain Space.
3. Chain 1 and make 3 DC in the next Chain Space.
4. Repeat steps 2 and 3 until you finish the whole row.
5. Slip stitch into your 1st stitch for this row.

3rd Row

1. Turn your work over and Chain 3 and make 2 DCs into the 1st Chain 2 space from the previous row.
2. Chain 2 and make 3 DCs into the same Chain 2 space.
3. Chain 1 and make 3 DCs into the next Chain Space.
4. Repeat step 3 once more, and then repeat step 2.
5. Keep doing step 3 and 4 until you complete this row. Finish off with a slip stitch.

You can make this Granny Square as big as you prefer, keeping in mind that you need to CH 2 for every "corner" to accommodate a larger amount of stitches, and to also turn it over after ever row. Again, maintain the tension so that you will not end up with a deformed Granny Square.

You can then join these squares with a tapestry needle to make an afghan, a bag, a trendy top, and a lot more. Your imagination and creativity will flourish with this easy and versatile motif!

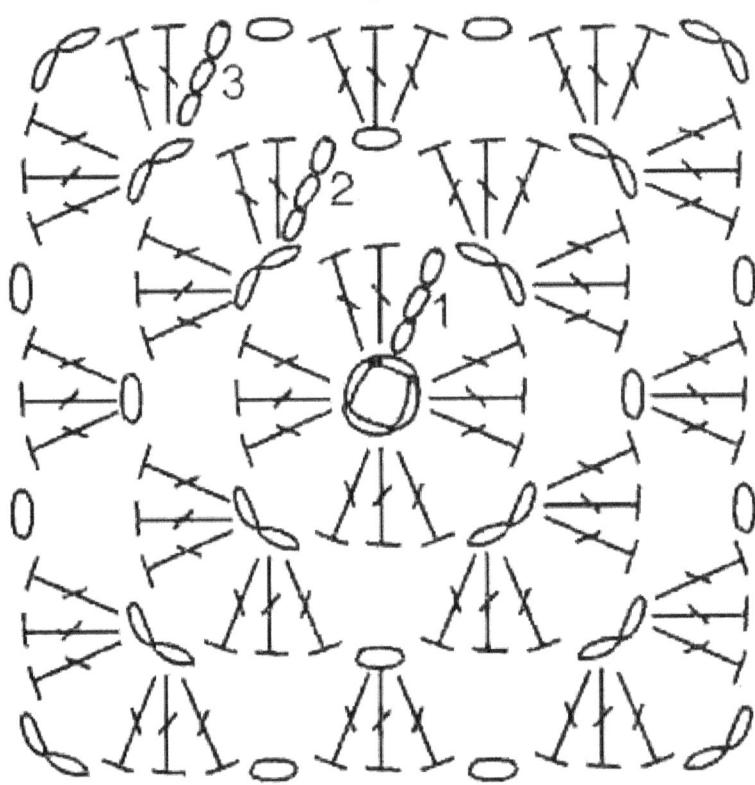

At Home

What makes a house a home? Aside from the people you love, a house becomes a home when you fill it with warm memories, trinkets, and things that you make from the heart. In the next few pages, let your personality and creativity flow in your home, by making these lovely crochet projects designed especially for your home.

1. Granny Crochet Blanket

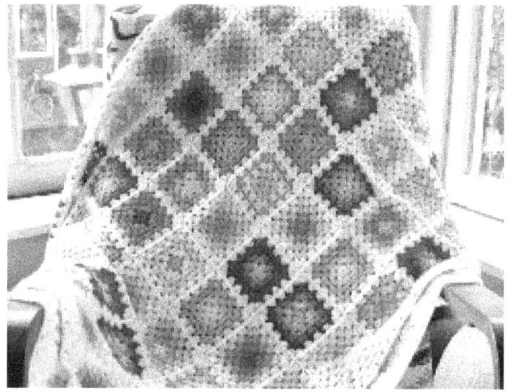

This is a long-term project. It's easy, but requires a lot of patience and commitment. If you think you're ready to make this gorgeous blanket, then let's get going!

Note: *This works well with any kind of yarn, just make sure you use the appropriate hook according to the yarn's thickness.* <u>It is important to check tension and maintain even stitches.</u>

<u>Here are some things you need to know before starting this project:</u>

- This blanket measures 40in x 69in or 100cm x 175cm
- Each Granny Square should measure 3.5in x 3.5in or 9 x 9cm
- You <u>need</u> to make ***135 Granny Squares*** for this project.
- You need to stitch or crochet together the motifs in 15 rows of 9

<u>Sample steps on how to connect the squares:</u>

1st Round

1. Connect joining yarn with a slip stich in any corner Chain Space with Chain 3, 2 DCs, Chain 3, and 3 DCs. In the same corner Chain Space, Chain 1

2. Make 3 DCs, and Chain 1 three times, and then make 1 DC in the next corner Chain Space, DC 2 together in the same corner Chain Space and corner Chain Space on next square, and 1 DC in the same corner Chain Space, then Chain 1.

3. Repeat step 2 for each square until you reach the other corner of the blanket.

4. Make 3 DCs, Chain 3, and 3 DCs in the blanket corner Chain Space, Chain 1.

5. Repeat from step 2 to step 4 for each side of the blanket, join with slip stitch in first DC, then fasten off.

2nd Round

1. Connect joining yarn with a slip stitch in any corner Chain Space, Chain 3, 2 DCs, Chain 3, and 3 DCs in same corner Chain Space, Chain 1.

2. Make 3 DCs and Chain 1 until you reach the next blanket corner Chain Space, make 3 DCs, Chain 3, 3 DCs in blanket corner Chain Space, Chain 1

3. Repeat step 2 for each side of the blanket, join with slips stitch in first DC, and then fasten off.

3rd to 4th Round

1. Repeat 2nd Round.

2. Maybelle Flower Coasters

Make these vintage crochet flower motifs into gorgeous coasters. Gradient, variegated, solid, or change colors for every row to make these coasters more personalized.

Note: *For this pattern, I recommend you use a chunky cotton yarn along with an appropriately sized hook.*

1st Round

1. Chain 10 and slip stitch into your 1st stitch to form a circle.
2. Chain 3 this will count as your 1st DC for this round.
3. Make 23 more DCs
4. Then slip stitch into your 1st stitch.

2nd Round

1. Chain 5 then SC into the 3rd stitch from the base of your chain.
2. Repeat step 1 until you finish this row.
3. Slip stitch into the 1st chain you made. You should have 8 half circles in total.

3rd Round

1. Slip stitch into the Chain Space.
2. In the same Chain Space, Chain 3 (this will be your 1st DC) make 1 more DC, Chain 2, 2 more DCs, and 1 Chain.
3. Repeat step 2 into all the Chain Spaces. Changing the 1st Chain 3

into 1 DC.

4. Slip stitch into the 1st stitch you made.

4th Round

1. Slip stitch your way into the 1st Chain Space of 2.
2. In the same Chain Space, Chain 3 and make 6 DCs, and 1 SC into the Chain of 1 from the previous round.
3. Make 7 DCs into the Chain Space of 2, and then 1 SC into the next Chain of 1 from the previous round.
4. Repeat step 4 until you've made fan stitches of 7 DCs into each Chain Space of 2.
5. Slip stitch into your 1st stitch, fasten off, and tuck in ends

3. Simple Mug Cozy

This lovely, simple, and useful project keeps my fingers from being burnt from the hot mug. Make it for yourself or give it to someone who is crazy for hot drinks!

Have fun making this!

Note: *This works well with any kind of <u>cotton</u> yarn, just make sure you use the appropriate hook for the yarn's thickness.*

Size may differ due to your mug's circumference. Measure it by making enough chains to go around your mug. Keep in mind that the chain will shrink a little when the SCs are stitched in.

1st Row

1. Make 55 Chains.

2nd Row

1. Make 55 SCs on each of the stitches from the previous row.

3rd to 7th Row

1. Chain 10, then SC into the 1st stitch.
2. Keep making 55 SCs on each of the stitches from the previous row.

8th to 12th Row

1. Chain 10, then SC into the 1st stitch.
2. Keep making 55 SCs on each of the stitches from the previous row.

13th to 14th Row

1. Chain 10, then SC into the 1ˢᵗ stitch.
2. Keep making 55 SCs on each of the stitches from the previous row.

Border

SC around your mug cozy to smoothen out the edges. Fasten off, cut excess yarn and tuck in the ends.

Stitch in 3 buttons—and you're good to go!

4. T-Shirt Yarn Basket

Have you ever worked with T-Shirt yarn before? This will be a great pattern to start off with! Even though this pattern works with any kind of yarn, I suggest you use a T-Shirt yarn.

Note: *This works well with any kind of yarn, just make sure you use the appropriate hook according to the yarn's thickness.* <u>It is important to check tension and maintain even stitches.</u>

1st Round

1. Start with making 3 Chains and slip stitching into the 1st stitch to make a ring.
2. Make 7 SCs into the ring.

2nd Round

1. SC 2 in each stitch. you should have 14 SCs when you finish this round.

3rd Round

1. Alternate making 1 SC in one stitch, and then 2 SCs in one stitch. you should have 21 SCs when you finish this round

4th Round

1. Alternate making 2 SCs in the next two stitches, 2 SCs in one stitch. You should have 28 SCs when you finish this round.

5th Round

1. Alternate making 3 SCs in the next three stitches, 2 SCs in one stitch. You should have 35 SCs when you finish this round.

6th Round

1. Alternate making 4 SCs in the next four stitches, 2 SCs in one stitch. You should have 42 SCs when you finish this round.

7th Round

1. Alternate making 5 SCs in the next five stitches, 2 SCs in one stitch. You should have 49 SCs when you finish this round.

8th Round

1. Make SCs in the back loops of each stitch. You should have 49 SCs when you finish this round.

9th to 16th Round

1. Make SCs around, maintaining 49 stitches for each round.

17th Round

1. Make 22 SCs then Chain 9 to make a handle, skip 3 stitches, SC in the next 21 stitches.
2. Chain 9 and skip 3 stitches again, to make the second handle.

18th Round

1. Continue making SCs around the rim.
2. When you reach the handles, SC over the stitches, making as many as needed to cover over the stitches from the previous round.
3. Slip stitch, fasten off and tuck in the ends.

5. Starburst Hotpad

This is a rather interesting take on boring hotpads. Make a few to spice up the look of your kitchen.

Functional and aesthetically beautiful, this hotpad is quite easy to make.

Note: *This works well with any kind of yarn, just make sure you use the appropriate hook according to the yarn's thickness.*

Reminder:

> ***DO NOT MAKE THESE HOTPADS OUT OF ACRYLIC YARNS. MAKE SURE THE YARN IS MADE OF COTTON.***

- You will need to make *five* of these motifs to achieve this hotpot.
- This will be much more eye-catching if each row is made using different colors.

You will need

- 4-ply **Cotton** worsted weight yarn
- Crochet hook G or 5-6mm
- Tapestry needle

1st Row

1. Form a ring by Chaining 5, and slip stitching into your 1st stitch.
2. Chain 3 (this will serve as your first DC), make 3 DCs into the ring—totaling to 4 DCs. After that, Chain 6. Make 3 more sets.
3. Having 4 sets of 4 DCs and 6 Chains, slip stitch the last stitch of your Chain into your 1st DC.

2nd Row

1. Chain 3 into the previous row's Chain 6, serving again as your 1st DC, make 11 more DCs into the same ring, totaling to 12 DCs.
2. Repeat step 1 until all 4 the Chain 6 from the previous row has a total of 12 DCs each.

3rd Row

You can go around this piece with a SC to make the shape more stable and to also add more color to it.

How to Assemble

Lay side by side, make sure the right side is facing you. Stitch them together in one corner, and so on, until you end up with a beautiful hotpad, same as the one in the picture. Make sure stitches are not visible, and tuck in ends.

Something to Wear

The next few pages are filled with clothing projects for cold winter days or warm summer days. The following projects are fast and easy to make.

1. Classic Puff Stitch Scarf

Make it in a solid color, gradient, or striped! I love crochet scarves, and no one should have just one! Make this scarf for yourself or give it to someone as a gift.

You will need

- 5mm hook
- Medium worsted yarn

1st Row

1. Start by making 26 Chain stitches.
2. Chain 3 and make your 1st Puff Stitch 1 Chain after the base of your Chain 3.
3. Make 12 Puff Stitches in total, with 1 Chain in between each.

2nd Row

1. Chain 3 and Continue making Puff Stitches in between the Puff Stitches from the previous row. Maintain 12 Puff Stitches per row, with 1 Chain in between each.

Keep going until you achieve your desired length.

Remember to always maintain 12 Puff Stitches per row, with 1 Chain in between each.

Add tassels at the end by cutting yarns in an equal length and attaching them by making a Lark's Head knot in the gaps between the Puff Stitches in the bottom ends of the scarf.

2. V-Stitch Infinity Scarf

Like I said, one can never have enough scarves! Try out this versatile scarf pattern. You can either make an infinity scarf or a regular one where you can add tassels. The length can be adjusted to your preference.

You will need

- 5mm hook
- Medium worsted yarn

1st Row

1. Begin by making 25 Chains.
2. DC into the 4th stitch from the hook. Chain 1 and DC into the same stitch to form a V. The 1st 3 Chains is your 1st DC for this row.
3. Skip 1 Chain from the previous row.
4. All in the same stitch, make DC, Chain 1, DC, and skip 1 stitch from the previous row.
5. Repeat step 4 until you finish this row.
6. Make 1 DC into the last Chain from the previous row. You should have 11 V-Stitches and 1 DC on each end of this row.

2nd Row

1. Turn your work over and Chain 3. Make V-Stitches into every V from the previous row, and then make 1 DC into the last stitch.

3rd to 80th Row

1. Repeat the 2nd Row until you reach the 80th Row.

2. To join each end, sew them together by making slip stitches.

3. Fasten off, cut, and tuck in the ends.

Note that this scarf is versatile and can be made as a regular scarf, or as an infinity scarf. It can be as long, or as short as you please. To achieve an infinity scarf, I suggest you make 80 rows or more, depending on your preference.

3. Virus Shawl

This interestingly named shawl pattern is easy and works up fast. There are many speculations, as to why it is named the way it is, but one thing is for certain—it is beautiful.

This pattern looks complicated, but is repetitive in an easy manner. So once you get the hang of it, it starts becoming easier to remember.

Note: *This works well with any kind of yarn, just make sure you use the appropriate hook according to the yarn's thickness.*

1st Row

1. Start with a slipstitch, and then Chain 10.
2. We will make a circle out of this, so link the end of your 10th Chain to the very first one.
3. Chain 3, and then do DC <u>into</u> the circle.
4. You now have 2 stitches. Continue making DCs into the circle until you have 20 DCs in total.

You want your DCs to form a U, and be flat as this is the middle of the triangular shawl pattern. So, bunch them up together and proceed to the 2nd row.

2nd Row

1. Turn your work over to the opposite side.

2. After the last double Chain, make 3 Chains. This will be considered your first DC in the 2nd row.

3. Make a total of 20 DCs on top of the first 20 you made.

3rd Row

1. Now turn your work over, and Chain 4 from the last DC.

2. In this row, we will start adding 1 Chain after each DC. Your 4th Chain will be considered your 1st Chain, as those 3 Chains before that are considered a DC.

3. Keep making DCs and single Chains alternatively until you reach the end of your semi-circle.

4th Row

This is where the pattern will start to emerge and become more interesting.

1. Turn your work over, and Chain 10 from the last DC.

2. Make a SC on the second Chain stitch.

3. Chain 4, and make a SC on the second Chain stitch from your last SC, do this step 3 times.

4. After the last SC, Chain 7 and then single stitch into the second Chain stitch. Make 2 of these.

5. Again, Chain 4, and make a SC on the second Chain stitch from your last SC, do this step 3 times.

6. After the last SC, Chain 7, and end this row with a DC into the last stitch.

5th Row

1. Turn your work over.

2. Make 3 Chain stitches after the DC. This will count as your 1st DC for this row.

3. After that, make 9 DCs into the Chain Space. Totaling to 10 if you count the 3 Chain stitches you made at the beginning.

4. Make a SC into the first small Chain Space, and then Chain 4

5. SC into the next small Chain Space, and Chain 4 again.
6. Make another SC into the last small Chain Space, and DC 10 into the big Chain Space that you come across.
7. After the 10th DC, continue with 10 more into the next big Chain Space.
8. Repeat step 4 and 5.
9. After the last SC, end this row with 10 DCs into the last big Chain Space.

6th Row

1. Turn your work over.
2. From the last DC from the previous row, make 3 Chains.
3. Make 9 DCs on top of the DCs from the previous row. Totaling to 10 DCs if you count the 1st 3 Chains you made.
4. Make a SC on the first small Chain Space, Chain 4, and then make another SC on the next small Chain Space.
5. Make 10 DCs on the previous row's 10 DCs.
6. After the last DC, continue making 10 more DCs on the next 10 DCs of the previous row.
7. Repeat step 4.
8. After that, end this row by making 10 DCs on top of the 10 DCs from the previous row.

7th Row

1. Turn your work over.
4. Same as the beginning of the 3rd row, Chain 4 from the last DC, because in this row, we will start adding 1 Chain after each DC. Your 4th Chain will be considered your 1st Chain, as those 3 Chains before that are considered a DC.
5. Alternately make DCs and Chains until you have 9 Chains and 10 DCs (including the first 3 Chains in the beginning) in total.
6. Repeat step 5 for the next 10 DCs from your previous row.

7. Only for this specific part, add 1 Chain before you repeat step 5 again.

8. End this row by repeating step 5 again.

8th Row

The 8th row will be similar to the 4th row, composed of big and small Chain Spaces to accommodate further expansion of the design.

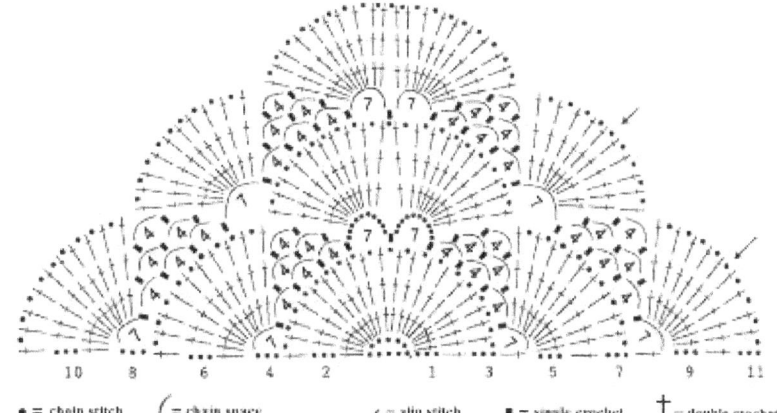

4. Granny Square Crop Top

Perfect for summer days on the beach! Since crop tops are trending again, I decided to include this pattern for the young and young at heart. This top is perfect to make for yourself, or as a gift to someone.

Note: *This works well with any kind of yarn, just make sure you use the appropriate hook according to the yarn's thickness.*

<u>As long as the measurement for each square's edge to edge is the same, it's going to be fine.</u>

You need to make 8 Granny Squares (*pattern found in this book*) that is according to your size (refer to size chart).

Remember to measure the squares edge to edge and not across.

Join the squares together however you like and add fringe by cutting yarns of the same length and attaching them to the bottom by making a Lark's Head knot.

Show off your creativity with this project. Do not be afraid to try new things!

Sizing	S	M	L	XL	XXL
Bust	34-36in	36-38in	40-42in	43-44in	46-48in
To join as is	6in	6.5in	7in	7.5in	8in
w/ Decorative border	5.5in	6in	6.5in	7in	7.5in
Strap Length	12in	13in	14in	15in	16in

5. Puff Stitch Beanie

Just like scarves, you can never have enough crochet beanies! Try making it with gradient or variegated yarn, and if you prefer beanies with big pompoms, you can add that, as well as other embellishments to make it more personalized to give it some color splash and character.

Have fun making this easy project!

1st Row

1. Make a ring with Chain 3, and then slip stitch into the first stitch.
2. In the ring, make 6 puff stitches and then join the last stitch with the 1st puff stitch.

2nd Row

1. In each gap—or Chain 1 spaces from the previous row—make 2 puff stitches in between. Making 12 in total.

3rd Row

2. In the first gap space or Chain 1, make 1 puff stitch, and in the next, make 2 puff stitches. Alternate between making 1 puff stitch, and 2 puff stitches until you finished this row. Having 18 puff stitches in total.
3. Slip stitch into the 1st puff stitch you made for this row.

4th Row

1. Alternate around this row by first making 2 puff stitches in the 1st 2 gaps, and then make 2 puff stitches in the 3rd gap. Alternate this

'two-1, one-2' until you finish this row. Having 24 puff stitches in total.

2. Finish off with a slip stitch.

5th Row

1. Alternate around this row with 1 puff stitch for the first 3 gaps, and then make 2 puff stitches on the 4th gap. Keep making this 'three-1, one-2' pattern until you finish this row. Having 30 puff stitches in total.

2. Slip stitch into the 1st puff stitch you made for this row.

6th Row

1. Alternate around t

2. his row with 1 puff stitch for the first 4 gaps, and then make 2 puff stitches on the 5th gap. Keep making this 'four-1, one-2' pattern until you finish this row. Having 36 puff stitches in total.

3. Slip stitch into the 1st puff stitch you made for this row.

7th to 15th Row

1. This time, only make 1 puff stitch for each gap. Having 36 puff stitches in total.

2. Slip stitch into the 1st puff stitch you made for this row.

16th Row

1. Chain 1, then SC in the 1st puff stitch from the previous row. It would help to put a stitch marker here. SC on each and every stitch from the previous row, including the gaps and the puff stitches. Do not slip stitch into the 1st stitch; instead, continue around until you have 72 SC in total.

17th to 19th Row

Keep making SC into each stitch until you reach the stitch marker on the 19th row.

Slip stitch into the following 2 stitches. Make sure to tuck in the ends.

6. Crochet Bow Ear Warmers

Keep those ears warm and toasty with these stylish ear warmers. The pattern is very straightforward and easy to understand. Try making this for yourself or make it for someone who needs to stay warm and cozy!

You will need:

- Worsted weight yarn or any bulky size 5 yarn
- 6mm Hook

Note: These instructions are for making an adult-sized headband with 20-22 inches circumference when done, and a width of 4 inches. It can be customized easily by removing or adding stitches to achieve the perfect fit.

Gauge: for the correct fit, make sure that for every 4 inches, you have 8 stitches for the right fit.

1st Round

1. Make 44 Chains and slip stitch into the first stitch to form a circle, being careful to not twist the loop.

2nd Round

1. Chain 3 (considering this your 1st DC)
2. Make 43 more DCs into each stitch.

3. Slip stitch into your first stitch in this round.

3rd Round

1. Chain 1 and SC in each and every single stitch.

2. Slip stitch into your 1st Chain for this round.

4th to 8th Round

1. Alternate between the 2nd round and 3rd round steps until you reach the 8th round.

2. When you reach the 8th round, and have slipstitched into your 1st stitch for that round, do not fasten off.

Loop yarn around the seam of the headband 6 times or more, depending on your preference. Slip stitch into the last stitch you made and fasten off. Tuck in loose ends.

7. 6-Size Double Pompom Beanie

This versatile beanie pattern comes in 6 sizes. For preemies, newborns, 3-6 months, toddlers, children, and adults. This does not have to end with a pompom on two sides, you can also just put one at the tip, or embellish with appliqués found in the last chapter of this book. Enjoy!

You will need

- Worsted weight yarn
- 5mm hook
- Tapestry needle

For this pattern, the beginning Chains in the beginning of each round will not be counted as stitches.

For Preemies: 4.25" to 5.5"

1st Round

1. Begin by making a Magic Ring.

2. Chain 3 then make 9 DCs in the Magic Ring.

3. Slipstitch into the 1st stitch you made in this round. You should have 9 DCs in total.

2nd Round

1. Chain 3

2. Make 2 DC in each stitch from the previous round.

3. Slipstitch into the 1st stitch you made. You should have 18 DCs in total.

3rd Round

1. Chain 3

2. Make 2 DCs into the same stitch and 1 DC into the next stitch.

3. Repeat step 2 until you finish this round.

4. Slipstitch into the 1st stitch you made. You should have 27 DCs in total.

4th Round

1. Chain 3

2. Make 2 DCs into the same stitch, and 2 DC into the next 2 stitches.

3. Repeat step 2 until you finish this round.

4. Slipstitch into the 1st stitch you made. You should have 36 DCs in total.

5th to 8th Round

1. Chain 3

2. DC around each stitch.

3. You should consistently have 36 DCs

9th Round

1. Chain 1

2. SC into each stitch from the previous round.

Slip stitch into your 1st stitch, fasten off, and tuck in ends.

For Newborns: 4.5" to 6"

1st Round

1. Begin by making a Magic Ring.
2. Chain 3 then make 10 DCs in the Magic Ring.
3. Slipstitch into the 1st stitch you made in this round. You should have 10 DCs in total.

2nd Round

1. Chain 3
2. Make 2 DC in each stitch from the previous round.
3. Slipstitch into the 1st stitch you made. You should have 20 DCs in total.

3rd Round

1. Chain 3
2. Make 2 DCs into the same stitch and 1 DC into the next stitch.
3. Repeat step 2 until you finish this round.
4. Slipstitch into the 1st stitch you made. You should have 30 DCs in total.

4th Round

1. Chain 3
2. Make 2 DCs into the same stitch, and 2 DC into the next 2 stitches.
3. Repeat step 2 until you finish this round.
4. Slipstitch into the 1st stitch you made. You should have 40 DCs in total.

5th to 9th Round

1. Chain 3
2. DC around each stitch.
3. You should consistently have 40 DCs

10th Round

1. Chain 1
2. SC into each stitch from the previous round.
3. Slip stitch into your 1st stitch, fasten off, and tuck in ends.

For 3 to 6 Months: 5.75" to 7.5"

1st Round

1. Begin by making a Magic Ring.
2. Chain 3 then make 11 DCs in the Magic Ring.
3. Slipstitch into the 1st stitch you made in this round. You should have 11 DCs in total.

2nd Round

1. Chain 3
2. Make 2 DC in each stitch from the previous round.
3. Slipstitch into the 1st stitch you made. You should have 22 DCs in total.

3rd Round

1. Chain 3
2. Make 2 DCs into the same stitch and 1 DC into the next stitch.
3. Repeat step 2 until you finish this round.
4. Slipstitch into the 1st stitch you made. You should have 33 DCs in total.

4th Round

1. Chain 3
2. Make 2 DCs into the same stitch, and 2 DC into the next 2 stitches.
3. Repeat step 2 until you finish this round.
4. Slipstitch into the 1st stitch you made. You should have 44 DCs in total.

5th Round

1. Chain 3
2. Make 2 DCs into the same stitch, and 10 DC into the next 2 stitches.

3. Repeat step 2 until you finish this round.
4. Slipstitch into the 1st stitch you made. You should have 48 DCs in total.

6th to 11th Round

1. Chain 3
2. DC into each stitch from the previous round.

12th Round

1. Chain 1
2. SC into each stitch from the previous round.
3. Slip stitch into your 1st stitch, fasten off, and tuck in ends.

For Toddlers: 6.75" to 8.75"

1st Round

1. Begin by making a Magic Ring.
2. Chain 3 then make 10 DCs in the Magic Ring.
3. Slipstitch into the 1st stitch you made in this round. You should have 10 DCs in total.

2nd Round

1. Chain 3
2. Make 2 DC in each stitch from the previous round.
3. Slipstitch into the 1st stitch you made. You should have 20 DCs in total.

3rd Round

1. Chain 3
2. Make 2 DCs into the same stitch and 1 DC into the next stitch.
3. Repeat step 2 until you finish this round.
4. Slipstitch into the 1st stitch you made. You should have 33 DCs in total.

4th Round

1. Chain 3
2. Make 2 DCs into the same stitch, and 2 DC into the next 2 stitches.
3. Repeat step 2 until you finish this round.
4. Slipstitch into the 1st stitch you made. You should have 44 DCs in total.

5th Round

1. Chain 3
2. Make 2 DCs into the same stitch, and 10 DC into the next 10 stitches.

3. Repeat step 2 until you finish this round.

4. Slipstitch into the 1st stitch you made. You should have 48 DCs in total.

6th Round

1. Chain 3

2. Make 2 DCs into the same stitch, and 11 DC into the next 11 stitches.

3. Repeat step 2 until you finish this round.

4. Slipstitch into the 1st stitch you made. You should have 52 DCs in total.

7th Round

1. Chain 3

2. Make 2 DCs into the same stitch, and 12 DC into the next 12 stitches.

3. Repeat step 2 until you finish this round.

4. Slipstitch into the 1st stitch you made. You should have 56 DCs in total.

8th to 13th Round

1. Chain 3

2. DC around each stitch

3. You should consistently have 56 DCs

14th Round

1. Chain 1

2. SC into each stitch from the previous round.

3. Slip stitch into your 1st stitch, fasten off, and tuck in ends.

For Children: 7.5" to 10.25"

1st Round

1. Begin by making a Magic Ring.
2. Chain 3 then make 10 DCs in the Magic Ring.
3. Slipstitch into the 1st stitch you made in this round. You should have 10 DCs in total.

2nd Round

1. Chain 3
2. Make 2 DC in each stitch from the previous round.
3. Slipstitch into the 1st stitch you made. You should have 20 DCs in total.

3rd Round

1. Chain 3
2. Make 2 DCs into the same stitch and 1 DC into the next stitch.
3. Repeat step 2 until you finish this round.
4. Slipstitch into the 1st stitch you made. You should have 30 DCs in total.

4th Round

1. Chain 3
2. Make 2 DCs into the same stitch, and 2 DC into the next 2 stitches.
3. Repeat step 2 until you finish this round.
4. Slipstitch into the 1st stitch you made. You should have 40 DCs in total.

5th Round

1. Chain 3
2. Make 2 DCs into the same stitch, and 3 DC into the next 3 stitches.

3. Repeat step 2 until you finish this round.

4. Slipstitch into the 1st stitch you made. You should have 50 DCs in total.

6th Round

1. Chain 3

2. Make 2 DCs into the same stitch, and 4 DC into the next 4 stitches.

3. Repeat step 2 until you finish this round.

4. Slipstitch into the 1st stitch you made. You should have 60 DCs in total.

7th Round

1. Chain 3

2. Make 2 DCs into the same stitch, and 29 DC into the next 29 stitches.

3. Repeat step 2 until you finish this round.

4. Slipstitch into the 1st stitch you made. You should have 62 DCs in total.

8th to 14th Round

1. Chain 3

2. DC around each stitch

3. You should consistently have 62 DCs

15th Round

1. Chain 1

2. Half DC into each stitch from the previous round.

3. Slip stitch into your 1st stitch, fasten off, and tuck in ends.

For Adults: 8.25" to 11"

1st Round

1. Begin by making a Magic Ring.
2. Chain 3 then make 11 DCs in the Magic Ring.
3. Slipstitch into the 1st stitch you made in this round. You should have 11 DCs in total.

2nd Round

1. Chain 3
2. Make 2 DC in each stitch from the previous round.
3. Slipstitch into the 1st stitch you made. You should have 22 DCs in total.

3rd Round

1. Chain 3
2. Make 2 DCs into the same stitch and 1 DC into the next stitch.
3. Repeat step 2 until you finish this round.
4. Slipstitch into the 1st stitch you made. You should have 33 DCs in total.

4th Round

1. Chain 3
2. Make 2 DCs into the same stitch, and 2 DC into the next 2 stitches.
3. Repeat step 2 until you finish this round.
4. Slipstitch into the 1st stitch you made. You should have 44 DCs in total.

5th Round

1. Chain 3
2. Make 2 DCs into the same stitch, and 3 DC into the next 3 stitches.

3. Repeat step 2 until you finish this round.

4. Slipstitch into the 1st stitch you made. You should have 55 DCs in total.

6th Round

1. Chain 3

2. Make 2 DCs into the same stitch, and 4 DC into the next 4 stitches.

3. Repeat step 2 until you finish this round.

4. Slipstitch into the 1st stitch you made. You should have 66 DCs in total.

7th to 15th Round

1. Chain 3

2. DC around each stitch

3. You should consistently have 66 DCs

16th Round

1. Chain 1

2. Half DC into each stitch from the previous round.

3. Slip stitch into your 1st stitch, fasten off, and tuck in ends.

Pompoms

Make 2 Pompoms that are as fluffy and as thick as you please. The fluffier, the better!

How to Assemble

Stitch two pompoms on either side of the beanie. Make sure it's positioned well before you stitch it in.

Crochet Appliqués

Have fun using all those scrap yarns on the projects we have mentioned in the next few pages! Make these appliqués for your crochet quilts, denim jackets, beanies, scarves, jeans, hair clips, and so much more! The possibilities are as limitless as your creativity.

1. Popcorn Stitch Flower

This easy, cute, and beautiful flower can be linked together to make rugs, headbands, or just for appliqués.

Note: *This works well with any kind of yarn, just make sure you use the appropriate hook according to the yarn's thickness.*

1st Round

1. Make a Magic Ring and SC 10 through it.
2. Slip stitch into the 1st stitch you made.

2nd Round

If you want to change colors for the petals, now is the time to do so.

1. Chain 3 and then make 4 Half DC into the same SC.
2. You should have 5 loops on your hook.
3. Keeping the 5 loops on, continue making 4 more Half DC into the next SC. You should have 9 loops on your hook.
4. Finally, with the yarn over your hook, pull it through all 9 loops on the hook.
5. Chain 3 and slip stitch into the next SC.
6. Repeat this step until you have 5 petals.

2. Classic Rose

This Classic Rose crochet is gorgeous for stitching on the side of a beanie, a denim jacket, on scarves, and so much more!

Note: *This works well with any kind of yarn, just make sure you use the appropriate hook according to the yarn's thickness.*

You will need

- Tapestry needle or any blunt needle.

1st Row

1. Leaving about 12 inches of thread for sewing, make 57 Chains.

2nd Row

1. Make a DC in the 6th chain from your hook, then Chain 2 and DC again into the same stitch.
2. Chain 2 and skip the next 2 Chains from the previous row, then DC, Chain 2, and DC again into the same stitch.
3. Repeat step 2 until you finish this row.

3rd Row

1. Turn your work over. Chain 3, this is considered your 1st DC. Make 5 DCs into the first Chain Space of 2, then make 1 SC into the next Chain Space of 2.
2. DC 6 into the next Chain Space of 2, and then 1 SC into the next Chain space of 2.
3. Repeat step 2 until you get 6 sets of these Fan Stitch of 6 DCs.
4. Now, make 9 DCs into the next Chain Space of 2, then SC into the

next Chain Space of 2.

5. Repeat step 4 until you have 5 sets of these Fan Stitch of 9 DCs.

6. Lastly, make 12 DCs in the next Chain Space of 2, then SC one in the next Chain Space of 2.

7. Repeat step 6 until you finish this row off, you should end with a SC in the last Chain Space.

8. Fasten off and leave a good few inches of yarn for assembling.

How to Assemble

Start rolling from the side where there are Fan Stitches of 6. Grab your tapestry needle, and start sewing it together. Keep rolling and sewing until you reach the end of the strip.

Once fully bunched together, tie both ends together tightly and securely. Tuck in the ends, and cut off.

3. Simple Heart Crochet

Here's another easy and beautiful appliqué for your crochet projects. Show some love with this crochet appliqué! This would look great scattered all over a child or a child at heart's jeans, on a beanie, or hair clips.

Note: *This works well with any kind of yarn, just make sure you use the appropriate hook according to the yarn's thickness.*

1st Round

1. Begin with a Magic Ring. Chain 3 and make 15 DCs into the Magic Ring.
2. Slip stitch into your 1st stitch. You should have 16 DCs in total.

2nd Round

1. Chain 2 and 1 DC into the same stitch.
2. Make 4 TRCs into the next stitch, and then 2 DCs into the next stitch.
3. Make 4 Half DC into the next 4 stitches.

We have now reached the bottom point of the heart.

4. Repeat step 3, all the way to step 1.
5. Slip stitch into the same stitch.
6. Fasten off, and tuck in ends.

4. Easy Bear

Are you looking for an easy to make bear for baby blankets, baby hats, baby jeans, or your patchwork afghan? I have the cutest and easiest bear pattern for you.

Note: *This works well with any kind of yarn, just make sure you use the appropriate hook according to the yarn's thickness.*

1st Round

1. Using a black yarn, begin with a Magic Ring.
2. Make 8 SC into the Magic Ring.
3. Slip stitch into the your 1st stitch and fasten off.

2nd Round

1. Using a brown yarn, Chain 3 and make 1 DC on the same SC from the previous round.
2. Make 2 DCs into the next SC, and so on, until you have a total of 16 DCs including the Chain 3.
3. Slip stitch onto the top of your Chain 3

3rd Round

1. Chain 3 and make 1 DC into the same stitch from the previous round.
2. Make 2 DCs into each stitch from the previous round.
3. Repeat step 2 until you have 32 DCs in total.

4th Round

1. Making a fan stitch, DC into the 2nd stitch to the left.
2. Make 6 more DCs into the same stitch to form the 1st ear.
3. SC into the 2nd stitch to the left.
4. SC into 6 more stitches.
5. Make the 2nd ear by making 7 DCs into the second stitch to left.
6. Finish off the second ear, by making a SC into the 2nd stitch to the left.
7. Finish the rest of the round with a SC to each remaining stitches until you reach the base of the 1st ear.
8. Slip stitch into it, and fasten off. Tuck away the ends. Stitch eyes with black yarn.

5. Basic Cherry

Adorable Cherry appliqués? I've got you covered! How adorable would these look on hairclips and anything denim?

Note: *This works well with any kind of yarn, just make sure you use the appropriate hook according to the yarn's thickness.*

Cherry Round

Make 2

1. Using red or any other preferred color, make a Magic Ring and make Chain 2.
2. Make 11 DCs.
3. Slip stitch onto your 1st stitch.
4. Fasten off the Magic Ring and tuck ends.

1st Stem

1. Slip stitch your green yarn into one of the cherry rounds and Chain 8.

1st Leaf

1. Chain 8
2. Flip your work and make 1 SC and 1 DC starting from your 2nd to the last stitch.
3. Make 2 TRCs, 1 DC and then SC.

2nd Leaf

1. Chain 8

2. Flip your work and make 1 SC and 1 DC starting from your 2nd to the last stitch.

3. Make 2 TRCs, 1 DC and then SC.

4. Slip stitch into the base of the 1st Leaf.

2nd Stem

1. Chain 8 and slipstitch into another Cherry round.

2. Fasten off and tuck in ends.

Keep in mind that you need to follow the order of the steps to achieve the look in the picture.

6. Simple Star

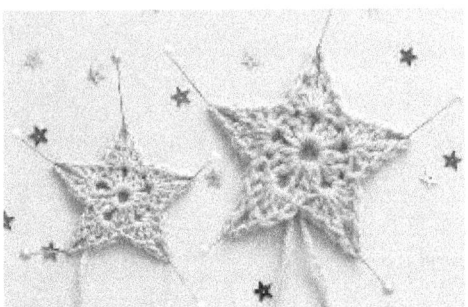

Simple with a grand look, this Crochet Star appliqué will be perfect for your next project.

Note: *This works well with any kind of yarn, just make sure you use the appropriate hook according to the yarn's thickness.*

1st Round

1. Chain 5. Make a slip stitch into your 1st stitch to make a ring.

2nd Round

2. Chain 3 and then make 2 DCs into the ring.
3. Chain 1 and make 3 DCs into the ring.
4. Repeat step 2 three more times, until you have 5 sets of 3 DCs with 5 Chain 1 in between.

3rd Round

1. Slip stitch into the next DC.
2. Into the 1st Chain Space to the left, make 2 DCs, 1 TRC, Chain 3, 1 TRC, and 2 DCs. After that, slip stitch into the middle stitch of the 1st set of 3 DCs to the left.
3. Repeat step 2 four more times to achieve a star.

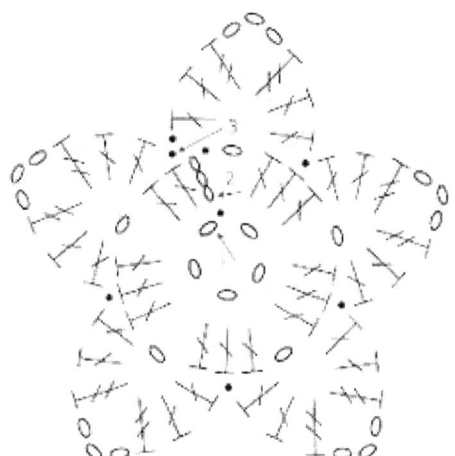

Conclusion

Crocheting is a fun craft to try your hand at. The learning curve is not steep as it only takes a few tries to get the hang of crocheting. Once you start, you will find yourself eager and interested in taking on bigger and more challenging projects. However, even the advanced projects are quite easy to master once you know the basics, so always have fun and if you feel like you've hit a roadblock, don't worry- just look back on this book or the patterns, and you'll be on the right track in no time. Good luck!